MORE PRAISE FOR *CAUSE FOR SUCCESS*

"When you Google *success* the first hit should be *Cause for Success!* This is a rare book — profiling interesting leaders, packed with useful knowledge, and well written and edited. Read it. Keep it close."

— John O'Neil, president of the Center for Leadership Renewal
and author of *The Paradox of Success*

"In the face of mounting evidence of a world in disequilibrium, the compelling stories in *Cause for Success* inspire hope. They are stories of visionary leaders who are redefining *normal* in the business world, creating and nurturing companies that serve society. They remind us that it really is within our power to walk more lightly on this earth."

— Liz Dowdeswell, president of
the Nuclear Waste Management Organization

"*Cause for Success* makes a compelling case that the great companies of the future will be companies that have integrated the motive for profit with the imperative to care about their community and the environment. The common good and private gain are not contradictions but complements for skillfully navigating an integrating world."

— Jim Garrison, president of the State of the World Forum
and author of *America As Empire*

"An inspiring, compelling, and highly readable set of stories about courageous corporate executives who have demonstrated beyond any doubt that social responsibility and a commitment to sustainability not only make the world a better place but also drive a better bottom line. This book will excite you about the powerfully positive role that corporate America is capable of playing in these perilous times."

— Tony Schwartz, author of *What Really Matters*

"*Cause for Success* demonstrates the power of innovation and leadership. CEOs who recognize the true costs of unfair or unsafe business practices to communities and the planet — and who therefore commit themselves to a better way — have actually built highly profitable and widely respected companies. By examining several well-known and widely regarded examples, the author effectively argues that it is in fact the commitment to do the right thing that has differentiated these companies and driven their success."

— Amy Domini, president of the Domini Social Equity Fund

"The way that businesses are run has a profound impact on the lives of pretty much everyone in the world, including those in the poorest countries. Christine Arena's book shows through the use of inspirational examples that companies and their leaders can establish a powerful new role for business in society. *Cause for Success* is an important call to arms for all business executives to recognize the vital responsibility they have in this world."

— Philip Rowley, president of AOL Europe

CAUSE FOR SUCCESS

CAUSE FOR SUCCESS

10 COMPANIES THAT PUT PROFITS SECOND AND CAME IN FIRST

How Solving the World's Problems
Improves Corporate Health,
Growth, and Competitive Edge

CHRISTINE ARENA

 New World Library
Novato, California

New World Library
14 Pamaron Way
Novato, CA 94949

Cover design by Mary Ann Casler
Interior design by Tona Pearce Myers

Library of Congress Cataloging-in-Publication Data
Arena, Christine.
  Cause for success : ten companies that put profits second and came in first : how solving the world's problems improves corporate health, growth, and competitive edge / Christine Arena.
      p.   cm.
  Includes bibliographical references and index.
  ISBN 1-57731-457-3 (pbk. : alk. paper)
  1. Social responsibility of business—Case studies. I. Title.
  HD60.A74 2004
  658.4'08—dc22   2004015443

First printing, November 2004
ISBN 1-57731-457-3

♻ Printed in Canada on 100% postcosumer waste recycled paper

g A proud member of the Green Press Initiative

Distributed to the trade by Publishers Group West

10 9 8 7 6 5 4 3 2 1

To my parents, Alice and Andy Arena

CONTENTS

ACKNOWLEDGMENTS

Cause for Success was not an endeavor I undertook alone. Michael Banks was my right hand. He was instrumental in getting the project off the ground, in keeping it afloat for over a year, and in helping me identify and recruit the very best corporate leaders to participate. Michael supported the project more than anyone else and for his assistance I am hugely grateful.

Marcia Polese, my cousin and esteemed business colleague, planted the seed for this book back in 2001 when she asked me the Po Bronson-esque question: "What do you want to do with the rest of your life?" My response and the subsequent guidance she offered led me to create the original book proposal. Without her encouragement, I may have never done so.

I was deeply honored to interact with this renowned group of corporate executives whom I consider heroes. Despite their schedules and professional obligations, these leaders patiently endured my in-depth interviews and follow-up conversations. In presenting their stories, each conveyed a devotion and passion I had not expected. To each of the following people, I would like to express my sincere hope that this book effectively portrays the enormity of your achievements. You are the trendsetters of twenty-first century business: Ray Anderson, Lord John Browne of Madingley, Dick Sabot, Amber Chand, Gary Hirshberg, Andrea Jung, Jeffrey Swartz, Bob Stiller, Anita Roddick, Dr. Muhammad Yunus, and Debra Dunn.

Numerous other people within the participating companies and related organizations were extremely helpful in enabling me to obtain and arrange the interviews, in responding to additional questions, and in providing me with critical documents and data. These people include Buddy Hay, Linda Sutton, and Janet Admunsen at Interface; Chris Mottershead, Nick Butler, and Heather Kingston at BP; Roddy Gow at Gow & Partners; Deborrah Himsel, Kathleen Walas, and Laura Castellano at Avon; Robin Giampa and Kate King at Timberland; Alan Khazei at City Year; Diane Davis and Betsey Stanford at Green Mountain Coffee Roasters; Steve McIvor, Helen Cocker, and Karen Bishop at The Body Shop; Alex Counts and Rob Sassor at the Grameen Foundation; and Liz Saiz and Kelly Ames at Hewlett-Packard.

This book took nearly a year to sell. It was passed over by multiple publishers who considered the topic too inspirational and woo-woo for commercial success in the business book category. Fortunately, there were several people who thought it could be a viable crossover project. Lisa Hagan, my literary agent, believed in the book from the very beginning and pushed it relentlessly. Jason Gardner, senior editor at New World Library, envisioned its potential and then made invaluable suggestions that brought the text, tone, and structure down to earth. Mimi Kusch, our copy editor, helped me to clarify key points. Without their guidance, this book would not be nearly as good.

Gene Miszack, the founder of Red Crest Entertainment, supplied me with the true opening story for the introduction. Gene, I wish you the best of luck in your endeavors. May you kindly make piles of money and prove the fools wrong.

The team at Polese Clancy — in particular Ellen Clancy, Sarah Heckles, Bruce Ployer, and Satvir Tib — provided additional assistance and designed our superb Web site and related materials, all of which demonstrate their first-rate creative and technical talents.

On a personal note, I must acknowledge an individual who helped me finish the book. Michael Donner offered me warmth, brutal honesty, intelligence, and constant comic relief. He tolerated my monk-like existence without complaint and kept things lighthearted all the way through. I am deeply indebted for his patience and understanding.

There are also others who listened to me drag on endlessly about my ideas and, each in their own way, helped me stay on track. These people include Simon Arena, Alice and Andy Arena, Marissa Arena, Alexa Arena, Maria and Bill Bell, Angela and Ned Foster, Amaya Rae, Gidion Brown, Karen Brown, Julie Nunn Martin and Rob Martin, Ozzy Gershon, Kristin Shannon, Sandra and Conrad Donner, David Speck, and of course, Sophie. Thank you all.

INTRODUCTION

The Rise of the
High-Purpose Company

Any invasion of armies can be resisted,
but not an idea whose time has come.

— Victor Hugo

"If you're going to build a company that truly serves society, you've got to be willing to experiment with new models," Gene, the head of a start-up media company, firmly told us as we were doing research for this book. "But try pitching those models to investment bankers. They will snub them before you can even justify their potential."

Like most start-up executives, Gene was in the midst of raising money for his firm. His meetings with potential investors had gone well, to a point. "Venture capitalists admire the solidity of our revenue, production, marketing, and distribution models. But when we reveal that products are designed to yield unusual social benefits, and that after certain revenue goals are met, profits will be split with the wider community, they turn cold. The retort is that such charity has no place in a business like ours, and that if investors want to make philan-thropic contributions, they should do so on the side."

Gene's predicament is common; corporate leaders are often hindered by this prevailing mind-set. Yet, as we illustrate in this book, the capitalist doctrine that a company's singular function is to make as much money as possible as quickly as possible — devoid of charity and divorced from society — is increasingly self-defeating. The less credence a company gives to the social and environmental inequities surrounding it, par-ticularly those inequities that *its* actions help to perpetuate, the less meaningful and invincible it tends to be. Inversely, the more a company operates with regard to the collective interest, the more it does something to improve people's lives and to solve society's problems, the more indispensable and sustain-able it ultimately becomes. *Cause for Success* shows that positive correlations exist between a company's wider sense of purpose and its health, its value, and its ability to endure.

In 1994 Paul Hawken, cofounder of garden retailer Smith & Hawken, convinced hundreds of thousands of people that industry was literally destroying life on earth. In his best-selling book *The Ecology of Commerce*, he noted a disturbing trend: as many of the world's gravest conditions — including the pollution of our air and water, the destruction of our forests, the rapid extinction of species, the deterioration of human health, the stress of the modern employee, and the widening rift between the rich and the poor — have worsened, business practices have grown progressively shifty and mal-adaptive. He predicted that this trend would eventually turn and that we would soon see a business transformation so sweeping it would render the commercial institutions of the future nearly unrecognizable.

Instead of operating divorced from society, or worse, at the expense of society, companies of the future would exist for the purpose of *restoring* society. They would thrive by rebuilding communities, repairing ecosystems, protecting the environment, improving human health, providing meaningful work, creating widespread prosperity, and enabling peace and security. At the time, naysayers interpreted Hawken's vision, and similar ones presented by other creative thinkers, as idealistic pipe dreams. But a critical mass of corporate leaders believed otherwise.

These leaders, including some highly influential CEOs, saw the flaws of an economic system that fails to take into account the costs companies create by doing business. They recognized that distinctions between how products are made and delivered and how, by their nature, products inflict harm, were conspicuously absent from the prices set in the global marketplace. For example, the costs of treating people who suffer as a result of the carcinogens in diesel exhaust are not covered by any of the industries that create that exhaust. Instead, society pays them. These leaders agreed that companies failing to address such "externalities" undermined their own long-term success. They reasoned that because of rapidly worsening social and environmental problems and the impact that those problems have on the whole of society — including business — voluntary evolution was a vital means of survival.

Today these corporate leaders drive one of the more interesting developments in the business world: the rise of the "high-purpose" company. A high-purpose company, as we define it, uses its greatest strengths to build social and economic value, to raise hope, and to extinguish despair. It exists to make a real and lasting contribution to society and considers profits a means to this end. Unlike the goals of traditional profit-driven enterprises, the charitable goals of high-purpose companies are so deeply ingrained in the genetic code of the organization that they drive innovation, stimulate growth and efficiency, and define corporate culture.

Rather than approaching social responsibility, environmental stewardship, philanthropy, operational accountability, and ethics as separate interests, high-purpose companies align the goals of these activities with their business strategies, leading them to become remarkably effective on all fronts. Though downplayed by the press, many high-purpose companies exist, and more are developing every day. In this book we focus on ten such companies, each of which demonstrates the use of different tactics for significantly improving world conditions while becoming more competitive at the same time.

Collectively, these companies represent a new era in capitalism. In this new era, service to humankind represents a key factor in business advancement. More companies are giving higher priority to the collective interest, not solely because they are altruistic, but also because they see how they can profit by doing so. In helping others, and in solving colossal world problems, they tap into unmet needs vital enough to sustain business performance over time. Each featured company has developed a market position, and in most cases, a revenue model that has direct and meaningful links to a social or environmental purpose. Each has a cause for success.

The corporations we discuss in this book may not be the ones you expect to read about. Some began and have grown their companies as exemplary corporate citizens, while others are recovering from severely blemished histories. Some are considered politically correct, while a few are controversial.

Despite their differences, each corporation represents an important lesson and a vital new approach. Through the insights, methods, and real-world experiences of the leaders driving each organization, we see how to identify the richest cause-related opportunities and to develop affirmative strategies for addressing these issues. We learn how to innovate in a sustainable direction, to adapt new standards of success, to elevate industry norms, and to transform our companies from within.

The evidence we present in this book is by no means comprehensive. Rather, we sought to explore a relatively untapped pool of knowledge that, once widely embraced, will force irreversible progress in the corporate world. A growing range of options is now available to companies ready to move their existing philanthropic efforts into more effectual territory. Naturally, since every company has its own set of social, environmental, and business goals, every approach will be unique. However, in evaluating the methods of our featured companies, we discovered some common themes that serve as a roadmap for those of you engaged in the process of evolving your business.

The companies featured in this book share the following key characteristics:

- *They are guided by compassionate leaders.* Capitalist convention suggests that there is no room for heart in business, but the CEOs we interviewed demonstrate that the opposite is true. Each leader exhibited an infallible social conscience and an ambition to see his or her ideas change the world. Nearly all were initially driven to transform their companies because of a powerful personal epiphany, experience, or change in belief system. Hawken's book awakened the conscience of

Interface's Ray Anderson and instigated his company's new sustainable business plan. An intimate brush with poverty during a business trip stunned Green Mountain Coffee's Bob Stiller and inspired his company's dedication to fair trade. A tragedy in Avon's Andrea Jung's family strengthened her company's resolve to finding a cure for breast cancer. These cases suggest that corporate transformation is fundamentally about *personal* transformation. Morally intelligent leadership created involvement and momentum within each company, leading to real and lasting progress.

- *They choose relevant crusades.* Each company recognized that it could create more value by supporting a cause directly related to its line of business. In solving pertinent social or environmental problems, these companies enhanced their ability to compete in some tangible way. Hewlett-Packard positioned itself for long-term growth by helping to raise the socioeconomic status of developing nations. Stonyfield Farm became a leader in the organic yogurt category by helping struggling dairy farmers to survive. By maintaining significant relevance to the core business, these companies fostered support from key stakeholders, enabling the companies to stay the course over time. In turn, this support not only made social and environmental results more profound and tangible but it also made business returns more achievable.

- *They walk their talk.* Instead of simply paying homage to their corporate values through mission statements and self-congratulatory press releases, each company transformed its charitable ideals into operational policies and practices. In each case, a distinct, articulated moral code served as the backbone and distinguishing factor of the company. Without a comprehensive focus on renewable energy, for example, BP would be just another oil giant. Lacking a motive to support developing countries, Eziba would be just another dot-com. These companies created a virtuous cycle of self-improvement. By aligning their philanthropic and business strategies, they rendered their social value and business values interdependent. The more progress they have made on the cause-related front, the more valuable their businesses have become.

- *They do something that no one else can.* Rather than relying on financial contributions as a primary means of support, each company uses its greatest strengths. Avon relies on its unique ability to build relationships in order to increase breast cancer awareness and advocacy. The Body Shop uses its talent for creative and persuasive communications to instigate widespread consumer activism. Timberland lends human capital, management expertise, and strategic skills to promote community volunteerism through its partner, City Year. Each company efficiently leveraged its core resources. And each applied business rigor and discipline to solving pervasive social and environmental problems. This combination led to the breakthroughs that continue to produce results.

- *They put the problem first.* Although each company wanted to get a financial return from its cause-related investment, that interest alone did not dictate the direction of the programs. Instead, each company took a needs-based approach. The Grameen Bank designed its banking system around the realities and constraints of its poverty-stricken clients. Hewlett-Packard custom-tailored a network of products, services, and business models to the challenging circumstances of emerging global markets. Green Mountain Coffee developed a coffee quality-control program that mitigates the hardships of coffee farmers in developing countries. By allowing the problem to lead to the appropriate solution, these companies discovered financially self-sustaining philanthropic models, while making their cause-related programs essential to the communities they serve.

- *They define success in broad terms.* Maximizing profits is still the ultimate goal of most corporate shareholders. However, our featured companies are equally determined to change the fate of the world. Unlike organizations driven by profits alone, these companies concentrate on creating long-term value and sustainability in all forms. Each has adopted new standards of success that incorporate environmentally and socially driven objectives, and most have begun to use new yardsticks in measuring their results. Interface, BP, and Stonyfield Farm attach financial value to their ecological impact on the planet. The Grameen Bank has established a performance review system based on the socioeconomic progress of its clients. By viewing success in terms of outcomes produced for the wider society as well as for themselves, these companies present a more complete picture of corporate health, both to shareholders and to the public at large.

With this rise of the high-purpose company, many of the firms we interviewed are just beginning to experience the fruits of their labors — profit. Even though each company could show a clear relationship between doing good and doing well, calculating a concrete, near-term financial return relative to social and environmental contributions remains a challenge. Several companies could quantify near-term financial growth through available market share and revenue data. In these cases, however, growth was a result of a multitude of variables, *including* the firms' social and environmental efforts.

These companies are seeking *long-term* success. They designed their programs to yield long-term returns, making their shorter-term returns both difficult to measure and relatively irrelevant to the success of the initiative. Every company was able to show considerable social or environmental results, and each experienced some form of meaningful business advantage. The bottom line was that they could all *qualify*, and in some cases *quantify*, the nature of those improvements.

The most commonly reported business benefits included:

- improved corporate health
- increased employee morale, retention, and productivity
- significant competitive edge
- improved customer loyalty and retention
- improved vendor and supplier relationships
- lowered overhead and operational expenses for those focused on environmental sustainability
- substantial opportunities for mid-term and long-term company growth

Certainly, each of these benefits includes a quantitative value as well. Companies save money by retaining customers and by attracting dedicated and highly motivated employees. They also profit from products and services that fulfill previously unrecognized needs. Unfortunately, these returns are not immediately apparent in quarterly reports. Furthermore, most companies simply do not comprehensively track the results of their charitable programs. This is a challenge for the industry, since companies are not required to publicly report their philanthropic spending, and even if they do so on their own, there are no industry standards for determining the value of their efforts. It is up to each company to determine the social and business value generated by its cause-related efforts independently, leaving some room for skeptics to question the worthiness of these endeavors.

Skeptics are right to ask why they should invest in cause-related programs. Too many proponents of corporate philanthropy and social responsibility believe that simply by investing in worthy crusades, companies will automatically profit. This is not so. As each of the following case studies shows, the relationship between environmental or social investment and shareholder value varies, depending on how the program is executed.[1] Ideally, a substantive business "reason why" exists.

In each case we reviewed, the business "reason why" was critical to the success and sustainability of the program. Without it, companies have difficulty sticking with the initiative over the long term, and the program becomes a peripheral interest that diminishes as soon as the company experiences a dip in revenues. The key is to make cause-related programs pay for themselves *over time*. Another key is *patience*, without which it is almost impossible for corporations to reap long-term rewards.

Fortunately, the cynicism that undermines the business merits of cause-related initiatives pales in comparison to the enthusiasm and passion of the corporate crusaders leading high-purpose companies. Their fierce convictions and extraordinary contributions are changing the course of business history. As more and more of these companies demonstrate results and share their experiences through books like this, investors will become convinced, corporate citizens will become inspired, and a significantly greater number of consumers will join the movement by supporting companies that put their noblest words into action. A day may come when purely profit-driven enterprises are hard-pressed to protect their market share against companies dedicated to worthier aspirations.[2]

These companies have had, and continue to have, a monumental impact on the world. They have affected the global economy and the fate of potentially billions of people. This is no exaggeration. So far these companies have helped to eliminate some of the world's most insidious diseases. They have unveiled enterprising solutions for saving the biosphere. They have inspired millions of consumers to protest against unfair business practices and to give back to their communities. They have raised tens of millions of people above the poverty line. They have provided these people with access to housing, electricity, sanitation, and clean water. More important, they have enabled them to enter the global economy as entrepreneurs, thus disbursing economic influence and opportunity more evenly throughout all levels of society.

These firms are effective not only because of their deeds but also because of the scope of their influence. They have inspired and, in some cases, forced, competitive companies, nonprofits, and other players around the world to follow in their footsteps. Their pioneering actions have created a tidal wave of positive, lasting socioeconomic change.

Each of the corporate leaders we interviewed for this book portrays a vision of the new business environment. In this environment, companies must deliver a concrete social value. They must serve a purpose greater than profiteering. Companies that practice unfairly or that operate without regard to the collective interest may survive in the short term. But long term, they are more likely to fail. Any company, regardless of size or industry, can further its success by approaching the world's social and environmental problems tactically.

In many ways, strategic corporate responsibility is the Internet of the early twenty-first century. It has created a new playing field with sophisticated rules. If well managed, it can mean the difference between a company's competitive advantage or disadvantage, its long-term growth or decline, and, ultimately, its success or failure. Unlike the Internet, however, the opportunities presented by strategic corporate responsibility are far easier to harness and pose greater long-term payoffs. It doesn't necessarily take millions of dollars, consultant expertise, or a sixth sense to successfully navigate a given company through these waters. Most companies already have everything necessary. All it takes, according to the corporate leaders we interviewed, is an ability to see a picture larger than a company's immediate reality, a desire to make a bigger difference, and a willingness to move forward.

Cause-related programs are not trivial side interests, but rich opportunities for business advancement.

CHAPTER ONE

CHANGING FACE

Interface • BP

It's not the strongest of the species that survives nor the most intelligent, but those most adaptive to change.

— Charles Darwin

Rather than resist change, Interface and BP chose to lead the evolution within their industries. They translated environmentally and socially responsible imperatives into business-building opportunities, thus successfully transforming themselves from challenged multinationals into model corporate citizens. Though their routes are unique, the results of their values-led efforts are similar. Both became more efficient and enterprising. Both achieved sustainable leadership positions. Furthermore, both created standards that continue to influence the global economy.

On August 31, 1994, Ray Anderson delivered a speech that dramatically altered the course of his life and the fate of his billion-dollar, publicly held company. As chairman and CEO of Interface, an Atlanta-based manufacturer of carpets, textiles, and architectural products primarily for the commercial interiors market, Anderson had enjoyed increasing success since founding the company in 1973. In just twenty-one years, he had grown Interface from a niche player to an industry leader. He now counted sales operations in 110 countries and 5,500 dedicated employees among his company's greatest assets. But just weeks before Anderson's speech, a few savvy customers began to ask tough questions about the company's environmental policies.

Typically, the Interface sales team responded elegantly to customer inquiries — particularly questions about performance, quality, and durability. But in seeking to respond to these unexpected requests for a thorough explanation of the company's environmental vision, the team was at a loss. "It was an awkward question," Anderson says. "Awkward, because we couldn't get beyond, 'We obey the law; we comply.'"[1] So rather than ignoring the inquiries and moving on to business as usual, the president of Interface's research arm decided to organize a task force to evaluate the company's worldwide environmental stance. Anderson was asked to deliver his speech to kick off the group's first meeting. Feeling completely unprepared, he reluctantly agreed. Anderson realized that he needed to educate himself on the issues that he and his company had so far disregarded — and fast.

Not knowing where to start, Anderson picked up Paul Hawken's renowned book *The Ecology of Commerce.* Before long he was floored: "The theory presented in that book hit me like a spear in my chest. I would lie in bed at night reading passages to my wife, and we would both weep together out of utter regret and the deepest sense of guilt." Through Hawken's book, Anderson absorbed several awful truths: that the earth's biosphere is in a long-term decline, that such decline is rapid and catastrophic, and that business and industry are largely responsible for the mess. "My business was a culprit, and I was a plunderer of the earth," he recalls.

It was a defining moment for Anderson, who realized that he could no longer run his company the same way. As he absorbed the wider implications of the unfortunate relationship between big business and the biosphere, he saw the world from a different perspective, one in which traditional capitalist tactics no longer seemed relevant. And so, on the day of his speech, Anderson presented his environmental task force with this new perspective and with a corresponding vision of an eco-friendly future for Interface.

> In twenty-one years we hadn't even thought about what we were doing to the earth. All we concerned ourselves with was whether or not there was enough raw material available for our products.
>
> — Ray Anderson

His message stunned everyone — including himself. Because of the disparity between his company's present and future course, the company had to be radically reinvented. Sourcing, procurement, product development, marketing processes, and research and development — all had to be aligned with a new and unusually ambitious goal. Starting immediately, Interface was to transform itself twice over — from an industrial "evildoer" to an environmentally sustainable company, and finally to an environmentally *restorative* company. Eventually, Interface would be the first name in industrial ecology worldwide, through action, not words.[2]

To an audience of seventeen awe-inspired yet baffled task force members, Anderson delivered this message with the intensity of someone who had just undergone a religious conversion. His vehemence was unlike anything they had come to expect from him. In the long run, Anderson's new fervor, radically heightened objectives, progressive thinking, and the management decisions that followed proved to be some of the best strategic moves the company had ever made.

> Some of my employees thought that it was a naive inspiration. Others wondered whether I had gone around the bend, so to speak. The truth is, I *had* gone around the bend to see what's there! That's my job.
>
> — Ray Anderson

At the time, Interface was the first United States–based industrial enterprise to take a comprehensive stand on environmental issues. Though many manufacturing companies talked about green initiatives, in reality the majority of their claims fell short. "Our competitors were doing zip," Anderson recalls. "We were the first in our category to face these issues comprehensively. I don't know of anyone else who has taken a more aggressive approach to solving environmental problems than we have." Anderson realized that the company's twenty-one-year practice of turning petrochemicals into carpets that last ten years and then spend up to twenty thousand years in landfills could neither sustain the planet nor jibe with a growing swell of consumer activism.

Today Interface owns the environmentally sustainable flooring market. Its eco-friendly policies stimulated a steady rise in market share, and the company is now the largest commercial carpet manufacturer in the world. In the nine years since Anderson's speech, the company's sustainable business policies have created new sources of revenue and allowed them to save more than $231 million in manufacturing costs. In addition,

Interface has been twice named as one of *Fortune* magazine's "100 Best Companies to Work For." It has also been hailed as "the most highly evolved big company in the country" and "the corporation of the twenty-first century."[3]

Anderson himself has achieved icon status, having been described in the media as "the greenest CEO in America,"[4] as "a certified captain of industrial capitalism," and as the kind of "radical who makes the folks from Greenpeace look timid."[5] He has received numerous awards and recognitions — including the National Academy of Science's Mitchell Prize, the first CEO recipient ever. To spur other industrial leaders into following his example, as of October 2003 Anderson had personally delivered more than 600 speeches on the topic of business sustainability and has written *Mid-Course Correction*, a book outlining the first four years of his company's transition.[6]

But perhaps Anderson's greatest legacy lies in his company's demonstration of "cyclic capitalism" — a form of commerce that works to renew itself while at the same time renewing rather than depleting its parent source, the earth. The concept is straightforward: for the past one hundred years, industrial capitalism has been uncompromisingly linear, extracting raw materials and energy to make products and packaging that generate vast quantities of waste.

Over the *next* one hundred years, Anderson wants industries to increasingly conserve raw materials and energy while recycling their own waste to feed the product cycle. Previously a negative side effect of the industrial process, waste now has the potential to become a viable profit maker for forward-thinking companies. Interface has many economists talking because it is one of the first living models of how and why cyclic capitalism works — and an even better example of what it takes to make such a shift.

OLD INDUSTRIAL ECONOMICS	NEW INDUSTRIAL ECONOMICS
Linear	Cyclical
Extractive	Renewable
Fossil-fuel driven	Hydrogen driven
Wasteful	Waste free
Focused on labor productivity	Focused on resource productivity
Abusive	Benign

The references above are taken from Ray Anderson's essay "Mindset." As of May 2004, this essay had not yet been published.

EXCERPTS FROM ANDERSON'S 1994 KICKOFF SPEECH

In the United States alone, some seventy thousand companies are already committed to some form of environmental commerce. We are in that group, but I do not think we are doing enough. We have not scratched the surface. We, and all businesses, have three issues to face: (1) what we take from the earth, (2) what we make, and (3) what we waste.

We must acknowledge the following: (1) We at Interface take oil from the earth in the form of nylon, latex, bitumen, and energy. And we don't put it back. We must push the envelope until we no longer take from the earth. (2) We make products that end up, at the end of their useful lives, in landfills, polluting the earth. We must push the envelope until nothing we make ends up polluting the earth. (3) We waste all along the way. Our industrial waste is a pollutant. We must push the envelope until all our waste is biodegradable and recyclable back into the food chain.

I believe it is good business, and will be increasingly so, to be stewards of the earth. Just as we know that quality doesn't cost, it pays, we must get to the point where stewardship (conservation) doesn't cost but pays. Our customers say they want it. Will they pay for it? We must see. We must give them the opportunity to tell us yes or no. It is a huge technological challenge. And a big management challenge too. The management challenge is doable quickly, I believe. We can begin by benchmarking among our own businesses. We can adopt best practices everywhere. Then our best practices become better and better, in Kaizen fashion.

We can focus our technological know-how — which is considerable, especially in the chemistry area — on breaking down the problem and parceling it out among ourselves, our suppliers, and our would-be suppliers. We have a lot of leverage, both with suppliers and would-be suppliers, to get them to join the process.

So the bottom line today is: let us commit with this kickoff to not just sit here, talking with each other, but to doing something. Specifically, doing what? I don't know. You must tell me when you're ready. I know you will figure it out.

I'm reminded of what a NASA scientist told us at a sales meeting years ago. President Kennedy's mission for NASA to put a man on the moon by 1969 turned out to be flawed. It was too easy. After Apollo XII, NASA floundered, looking for a suitable new mission. So let's make our mission ambitious enough.

How about this for a mission: to convert Interface into a restorative enterprise, worldwide. How about this for a strategy: to reclaim, reuse, recycle, conserve, adopt, and advance best practices. And how about this for a goal: to achieve sustainability by _____. You must fill in the year. In fact, feel free to take each of these, massage them, develop them, then come back to me with your version of each.

Thank you for this beginning. I know it will lead to good things. All the best.

CHANGING FACE

Many companies find themselves in an awkward position, stuck between their convictions and their actions, between notions of what *can* be done, given their resources, and what *should* be done, given their ideals. In most cases, the source of this stagnancy is fear — of the unknown, of not meeting quarterly goals, of disrupting proven processes, of being ridiculed by industry analysts. If you asked Ray Anderson, he would tell you that the key to overcoming these kinds of fears is facing the whole truth and that doing so can enable a full-fledged corporate turnaround.

"Though they were very painful at times, our internal discussions yielded a totally new worldview," Anderson remembers. "We realized not only that our old business approach was upside down, but also that most economists had it wrong too. The economy is a wholly owned subsidiary of the environment. It's not the other way around." By owning up to the company's past infractions and acknowledging its role in a larger, interrelated economic and environmental system, Anderson created a psychological shift that galvanized his workforce. "I remember the watershed moment," Anderson says. "I was presenting my vision to our European contingency, and many in the audience were skeptical. After the speech was over and the group dispersed, I found one of my European managers sitting alone in the auditorium with a copy of my transcript in his hand. He was clearly emotional. He looked up at me and said, 'I've heard this before, but I just want you to know that I get it now.' I realized that the shared sense of distress over what we and companies like us had been doing would serve as the basis of our transformation." Instead of dwelling on the past, Anderson and his team became charged by it.

A company's successful rebirth into true social responsibility requires rare leadership. A distinct combination of rational, emotional, and moral intelligence is key. If the CEO doesn't fully "get it" intuitively, then no one will. The magnitude of environmental or social consequences of the current business course must inspire in him or her an urgency to respond. Turnarounds require an authentic spark from the top. But if the first step toward corporate rebirth is revelation, the next crucial step is steadfast communication, as the arduous task of convincing employees, shareholders, customers, and suppliers follows. For Interface, this meant convincing each group to go about things in an entirely new way.

> The economy is utterly dependent on the environment, and it is utter stupidity that we keep fouling the source of our wealth. The environment is the goose laying the golden egg, and we're ruining it.
>
> — Ray Anderson

ISSUING PARTICIPATION

Anderson made three key decisions that enabled his company to move forward. First, to sell his vision to stakeholders, he implemented a communications strategy that was akin to a political campaign. "I took every available opportunity to talk to people," he says. "I did sales and factory meetings. I talked to people individually. I addressed the supply chain directly, and I gave keynote addresses at international events. I did this for nine years, and I'm still going."

Knowing that with each audience he might face significant resistance, Anderson customized his messages, speaking directly to each group's ambitions and misgivings. Anderson approached each group incrementally — starting with employees,

HOW ANDERSON GAINED STAKEHOLDER SUPPORT	
WINNING EMPLOYEE ADVOCACY	"I started with a core group of seventeen task force members and asked them to go back into their businesses and figure out ways to bring their teams closer to the new goal of company-wide sustainability. This transference of ownership from me to them created great momentum. From then on, every group I engaged with was given the same charter — which gave rise to innovation and in general enabled a very sharp focus."
WINNING SUPPLIER ADVOCACY	"I spelled out the new vision, and then basically said, 'Either come with us, or don't.' Luckily, their response was 'Okay, help us understand what you mean. We're with you.' In some cases, the outcome of our shared commitment to sustainability has changed the nature of their business as well as ours."
WINNING SHAREHOLDER ADVOCACY	"We [senior management] were hesitant to talk to shareholders at first because we weren't sure how to approach the issue of 'doing the right thing.' Ultimately, we created an initiative called QUEST, where we had a firm dollar metric to present as an indicator of the value and cumulative savings we had achieved through sustainable activities. That went down very well."
WINNING CUSTOMER ADVOCACY	"We had to establish a strong bond of trust. We did this through a strict policy of not foisting an inferior product onto customers in the name of sustainability. We were able to look customers in the eye and say, 'We need you to support our effort, and we'll never take advantage of you in return.' In addition, I gave a great many public speeches that have lifted our image in the eyes of the public."

then suppliers, then shareholders, and finally customers — until he had built the necessary momentum and critical mass of support.

Anderson's second crucial decision was to pass ownership of the sustainability strategy from himself, as the visionary, to his audience, the implementers. He looked to employees, suppliers, shareholders, and even customers for the necessary ideas, solutions, and support rather than choosing a course of action by himself and directing others to follow. "This was key," Anderson says, "because everyone went back to their respective businesses and just started agitating. And that's where you start. That's how you *do* something, anything, to get started."

Anderson communicated the damage the company's classic industrial model of "taking, making, and wasting" had done as simply and directly as he could, while also leveraging Interface's presence. "We are big enough to make a difference, especially when our entire supply chain is engaged," he says. The company relies on such industrial partners as DuPont, Exxon, Solutia, Goodyear, and BASF to make its product cycle work, and Anderson depended on them to recognize the business potential associated with leading industry-wide shifts to more progressive environmental policies.

Anderson also purposefully harnessed the purchasing power of his customers. He understood that if he could convince them to follow along, Interface could dominate the sustainable commercial interiors category — thus forcing competitors to follow suit and slowly changing the industry as a whole. "Our customers are the largest corporations, the biggest hospitals, the largest government agencies, the finest universities, and the busiest airports in the world," he writes. "These fertile conditions just do not exist in very many corporations, and that is why the 'do' factor is so low."[7]

The third crucial decision that Anderson made was to invest heavily in team building. An ongoing series of employee training programs, which are still under way, set the stage for product and process innovations — the results of which Interface now takes to the bank. "We focused a great deal on letting go of old ideas, embracing risk, being willing to take chances, and learning that you can't do it on your own. Out of this, we became a more tightly knit company. The effect of our training approach is that most everyone within the company understands what their role is." Although Anderson admits that the vision still hasn't completely penetrated the company, he adds, "Today if you picked someone off of the product line, they would most likely start talking about sustainability."

TAKING INCREMENTAL STEPS

Change at Interface began as more of a trickle up from below than as a big surge from the top, as small innovations eventually led to larger, system-wide improvements. One of the first ideas came from factory plant managers, several of whom began reusing rather than discarding their carpet trimmings. They ended up preventing more than three million pounds of practically indestructible, nonbiodegradable nylon carpet scrap from being sent to landfills — per factory, per year.

> We focused on waste reduction and redefined quality as an absence of waste in any form. Very soon, this became the basis of everything we did. You could say that we ate the elephant one bite at a time.
>
> — Ray Anderson

Other Interface divisions began to tell similar stories. For instance, in one of the company's best innovations, the sales team decided to transform the way carpet was sold. Instead of customers purchasing Interface carpet the usual way — buying it, using it for ten years, and then throwing it away — Interface would lease its carpet, enabling the company to take back its products at the end of their cycle, disassemble them, and remake them back into new products.

Another bright idea came from the product development group. They resolved to remove one ounce of nylon per square yard of carpet, which comprised about 4 percent of the average Interface carpet's total face weight, and see how the product held up under performance tests. To the group's delight, product quality remained the same, and so the change was implemented. "The reduction of an ounce of nylon per square yard got to be a big thing," Anderson says. "We discovered that by doing so we saved enough energy upstream to power our factory for two years." Innovations like these continued to unfold across the company, giving rise to broadening policies and eventually to a far more explicit strategy.

At Interface, sustainability didn't just mean environmental advocacy; it meant continually improving operational efficiency, thus improving shareholders' return on investment and enhancing long-term company health. To permanently hold the company to this robust vision of sustainability, Anderson implemented the Seven Fronts, a design model that addressed every aspect of the company's operations.

INTERFACE'S SEVEN FRONTS

1. Eliminate waste. **2.** Generate no harmful emissions. **3.** Use renewable energy sources. **4.** Achieve closed-loop recycling. **5.** Use resource-efficient transportation. **6.** Engage and sensitize stakeholders. **7.** Pioneer sustainable commerce.

Through Seven Fronts, Interface would waste less and therefore spend less. It would consume less raw material, and therefore carry less inventory. It would streamline production, and thus use less energy.[8] In addition to improving the company's existing products and processes, the Seven Fronts approach led to some considerable breakthroughs, including the creation of new 100 percent recycled content product lines and of nonrecycled products made for easy disassembly and eventual reuse, as well as the sourcing of revolutionary and environmentally sound materials such as polylactic acid (a new fiber technology derived from corn) and hemp. Interface's eco-sensitive products ended up performing better in the market-place and are still considered some of the most unique and aesthetically pleasing in the industry.

Since implementing the Seven Fronts, Interface has relied on the ideas behind cyclic capitalism to drive its sales and profits. In general, the past eight years at Interface have shown that increasing efficiency both bolsters social and environmental responsibility and delivers better value to customers and shareholders. Yet the transition from a linear to a cyclic economic model has not been entirely smooth. The company did experience a bump along the way when the industry lost momentum and skeptics began to question the viability of a truly sustainable industrial corporation.

FACING DIFFICULT TIMES

During the fourth quarter of 1998, two years after Interface initiated the Seven Fronts approach, the commercial interiors industry turned soft. As customers woke up to the supposedly dire technological implications of Y2K, corporate funds were hastily reallocated to reconfiguring computer systems. Carpet was the last thing on anybody's mind. "Y2K really sucked the life out of our marketplace," Anderson remembers. "Shortly afterward there was a nice rally, but then came the dot-com bust in 2000, and we've been operating in the worst environment our industry has faced in thirty years ever since. Financial performance has been miserable. Even though we have come back, we are still way below our peak."

INTERFACE'S NET SALES (IN THOUSANDS)				
2003	2002	2001	2000	1999
$923,509	$924,084	$1,058,846	$1,283,948	$1,228,239

Despite a three-year dip in revenues, Interface has taken aggressive steps to become more productive and efficient — without diminishing its focus on sustainability. As the company vehemently asserts to critics and shareholders in its annual reports, it is in fact now more productive and better poised to take advantage of an imminent economic and category upswing. Recent signs point to a growth trend for the company, as sales improvements have surfaced for the past four quarters in a row. Its first-quarter 2004 earnings were $249.2 million, compared with $210.2 million the previous year.

Looking behind the numbers is essential to understanding the whole picture at Interface — that is, how Interface's Seven Fronts have affected overall company health. In addition to the company's restructuring and new marketing

> Some people have asked me, 'If you had to do it all again, would you have continued to pursue sustainability in light of declining profit?' My answer is, hell, yes! Sustainability has been our salvation. We have never had one thought about turning back.
>
> — Ray Anderson

efforts, there are other encouraging signs. First, while the commercial interiors market as a whole has shrunk between 25 and 40 percent during the past three years, Interface has gained significant competitive advantage and experienced overall improvements in several key areas of its business. "What we can offer, better than any other company in the world, is modular carpet," Interface's current CEO Daniel T. Hendrix writes. "And modular [a more cost and eco-efficient carpet solution] is poised to explode across every market segment and around the globe."9 In addition, while many competitors have remained low profile over the past five years, Interface has amplified its presence and seized untapped market opportunities. As a result, the company has increased overall market share. Finally, Interface continues to develop more efficiently and to yield higher margins owing to its focus on sustainability. "We would be far worse off had we not been following a sustainability path," Anderson says. "The savings we've gained have been crucial, and the goodwill in the marketplace has won us business we otherwise might have lost. From the top line through the bottom line we have benefited, while a number of our competitors have gone out of business."

NEW MEASURES

Interface has defined for the entire industrial world new notions of sustainability, prosperity, and capitalism itself. "It's about processes, people, profits, products, and purpose — all growing out of the proper respect for the environment, the earth, and the people who live here," Anderson says. Though the company's business approach continues to progress, Anderson has stuck to his grand plan, which has allowed for unprecedented achievements.

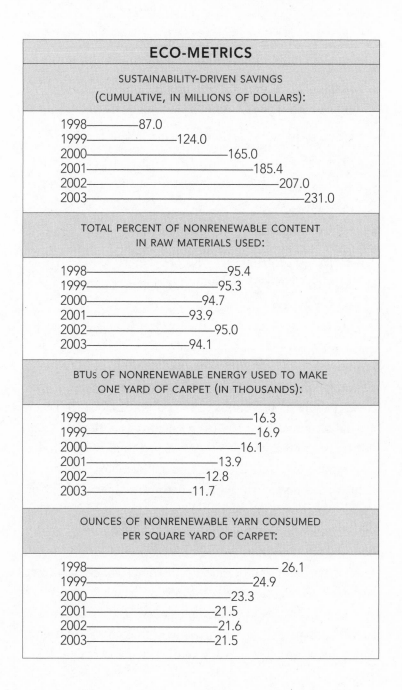

ECO-METRICS

SUSTAINABILITY-DRIVEN SAVINGS
(CUMULATIVE, IN MILLIONS OF DOLLARS):

1998————87.0
1999————————124.0
2000————————————165.0
2001——————————————185.4
2002————————————————207.0
2003——————————————————231.0

TOTAL PERCENT OF NONRENEWABLE CONTENT
IN RAW MATERIALS USED:

1998————————————95.4
1999————————————95.3
2000——————————94.7
2001————————93.9
2002——————————95.0
2003————————94.1

BTUs OF NONRENEWABLE ENERGY USED TO MAKE
ONE YARD OF CARPET (IN THOUSANDS):

1998——————————————16.3
1999——————————————16.9
2000————————————16.1
2001————————13.9
2002——————12.8
2003————11.7

OUNCES OF NONRENEWABLE YARN CONSUMED
PER SQUARE YARD OF CARPET:

1998————————————————— 26.1
1999——————————————24.9
2000————————————23.3
2001————————21.5
2002————————21.6
2003————————21.5

Since 1996 Interface has

- reduced its manufacturing costs by approximately 20 percent per dollar of sales;
- reduced the volume of scrap materials sent to landfills by 79 percent;[10]
- reduced its carpet factory water consumption by 56 percent;
- reduced its overall energy consumption by 31 percent;[11]
- reduced its global greenhouse gas emissions by 29 percent;
- reduced its petroleum-based raw materials consumption by 28 percent.[12]

For any challenge the company faces, or for any creative breakthrough the company wishes to make, Interface looks to nature for the solution. The evolution of the company's processes, people, profits, products, and purpose follows the laws of natural selection. Their success results from continually adapting to any given environment. "We've had to redefine ourselves many times over the years — through economic downturns, industry movements, the bursting of the technology bubble, and the aftermath of September 11," Hendrix says. "And we've risen to the challenge every time, reinventing and relearning our business, and always coming out the better for it."[13]

But far more significant than just improving itself, Interface has bettered the overall economy by challenging the mindset behind it. "Prosperity at the expense of the environment is fake prosperity — worse than Enron's or Worldcom's," Anderson writes. "Or, to put it another way: What CEO, given a subsidiary that required a constant and continual infusion of capital just to keep it going, would keep that subsidiary? None that I know. Nature is a better manager than any CEO I know, and capable of being far more ruthless if she needs to be."[14]

ROUSING A GIANT

If Anderson's task of transforming a challenged $1 billion manufacturing company into a model corporate citizen seems grueling, imagine redirecting a $179 billion empire in a politically scrutinized industry notorious for causing environmental degradation. This is precisely what Lord John Browne of Madingley, British Petroleum PLC's group chief executive, has set out to do.

Browne, whose vision has helped BP grow from an oil company into a global leader in clean energy and eco-conscious business practices, has an unconventional personal history compared with other CEOs. At sixteen he began serving BP as an apprentice and gradually moved up through the ranks. During his climb, he managed to earn degrees from Cambridge University and Stanford University's graduate School of Business. He finally took his post as group chief executive in 1995. Three years later, Browne was knighted by the Queen of England. Today he is regarded as one of Europe's gutsiest and most influential corporate leaders.

As head of BP, Browne has made several industry-shaking statements. The most dramatic of these occurred in 1997 at his alma mater, Stanford Business School. Before a crowd of graduating students, faculty, and journalists, Browne acknowledged what other oil industry leaders previously had refused to talk about, let alone admit. Global warming, he said, was indeed a problem, and it was essential that companies take precautionary measures to address the long-term risks of climate change.

While his proclamation came as a welcome surprise to some, others considered it nothing short of blasphemous. Browne had crossed political lines and broken with traditional petroleum industry ranks. He had forced competitive companies — most of which resisted the idea of mandated limits to greenhouse gas emissions — to publicly defend and proactively address their own environmental policies. Browne, in his restrained and dignified way, downplays the initial range of reaction: "Many people were supportive, others were understandably skeptical, while a few were antagonistic."

> While some of our competitors were not convinced by scientific arguments regarding climate change, others were. We crystallized an increasingly held view that prudent action was necessary.
>
> — Lord John Browne

Browne went on to announce that, in response to clear evidence of climate change, BP would work to reduce its CO_2 emissions to 10 percent below 1990 levels by 2010 and invest heavily in renewable energy sources such as solar power. His proposal was immediately hailed by the press as "a maverick position in the oil industry,"[15] "a break as stunning as that which shook the tobacco industry,"[16] and "the most positive response [to the environment] by an oil company."[17]

Some environmentalists mocked BP's stance, claiming the new targets did not go far enough and thus "lack[ed] environmental credibility."[18] At the same time, competitors asserted that "efforts to limit the release of greenhouse gases could severely disrupt economies and later turn out to be unnecessary."[19] At an oil industry conference a few months after Browne's speech, Senate Majority Leader Trent Lott joined in the backlash, belittling BP's pledged focus on alternative energy: "This is the hippies' program from the seventies, and they're still pushing this stuff."[20]

Today BP continues to encounter critics at every turn. With its progressive proposals, the company serves as an easy target both of conservatives who resist change and of environmentalists who suspect ulterior motives. Browne doesn't expect the company's detractors to pull back anytime soon. He does, however, recognize why the company consistently attracts such opposition: "Sometimes [critics test us] to gain reassurance that we are living up to our commitments, sometimes because there is misunderstanding, and sometimes because they have seen opportunities that did not occur to us. Occasionally, people make complaints against us because we provide a platform and visibility for their own campaigns."

> Our progressive position created an expectation that we will strive to achieve constant improvement, and we should not be surprised when people test this resolve.
>
> — Lord John Browne

Despite this skepticism, BP leads the industry in policy, practice, and performance. Since Browne presented the company's 1997 environmental pledge, BP has met its 10 percent CO_2 reduction goal — nine years ahead of schedule. In addition, since Browne announced the company's transition, BP's revenues have climbed from $109 billion to $179 billion, while the company's environmental efforts have directly generated $650 million worth of value on a $20 million investment.[21] Meanwhile, the company's stock price has tripled, and BP has twice produced the largest quarterly profit reported by any company in recent history. BP is now the world's second largest energy giant, the world's second largest producer of solar panels, and the world's leading supplier of cleaner-burning fuels.

However, as Browne willingly acknowledges, the company still has far to go — as the shift from oil and natural gas and renewable resources cannot possibly happen overnight. Like Interface, BP relies on petroleum resources, and thus the nature of its business creates negative externalities. Every day, it drills for oil in ecologically sensitive areas. Last year, it released 80.5 million tons of CO_2 into the atmosphere. It also reported 742 separate incidents of oil or chemical spills of at least one barrel or more. Then again, in addition to decreasing CO_2 emissions by some 14.7 million tons since 1998, the frequency of oil and chemical spills was 30 percent lower in 2002 than in 1999, indicating an improving trend. Also, like Interface, BP continues to outshine its competition by voluntarily setting ever more aggressive environmental and safety targets each year and by consistently delivering on its promises. Whether or not critics acknowledge it, BP, because of its actions and influence on the industry as a whole, is a corporate leader in environmental progress.

To discount the whole of a company's achievements based solely on its imperfections or on its history in an environmentally damaging business would be a grave mistake. During the past six years, BP has presented us with powerful lessons on how a company of enormous scale and influence can begin to serve both the greater good and shareholder interests at the same time. And this understanding is key to the evolution of the corporate world.

EXCERPTS FROM BROWNE'S 1997 "CLIMATE CHANGE" SPEECH

There is now an effective consensus among the world's leading scientists and serious and well-informed people outside the scientific community that there is a discernable human influence on the climate, and a link between the concentration of carbon dioxide and the increase in the temperature. It would be unwise and potentially dangerous to ignore the mounting concern.

The time to consider policy dimensions of climate change is not when the link between greenhouse gasses and climate change is conclusively proven, but when the possibility cannot be discounted and is taken seriously by the society in which we are part.

We in BP have reached that point. It is an important moment for us. A moment when analysis demonstrates the need for action and solutions.

What we propose to do is substantial, real, and measurable. I believe it will make a difference. We're taking some specific steps to control our own emissions, to fund continuing scientific research, to take initiatives for joint implementation, to develop alternative fuels for the long term, and to contribute to the public policy debate in search of the wider global answers to the problem.

Nobody can do everything at once. Companies work by prioritizing what they do. They take the easiest steps first — picking the low-hanging fruit — and then they move on to tackle the more difficult and complex problems. This is the natural business process.

Our method has been to focus on one item at a time, to identify what can be delivered, to establish monitoring processes and targets as part of our internal management system, and to put in place an external confirmation of delivery. In most cases the approach has meant that we've been able to go well beyond the regulatory requirements.

No company can be really successful unless it is sustainable — unless it has the capacity to keep using its skills and to keep growing its business. Of course, that requires a competitive financial performance. But it does require something more, perhaps particularly in the oil industry.

To be sustainable, companies need a sustainable world. That means a world where the environmental equilibrium is maintained but also a world whose population can all enjoy the heat, light, and mobility which we take for granted and which the oil industry helps to provide.

I don't believe those are incompatible goals. Everything I've said today — all the actions we're taking and will take are directed at ensuring that they are not incompatible. There are no easy answers. No silver bullets. Just steps in a journey which we should take together because we all have a vital interest in finding the answers.

BP'S PATH TO GREENER PASTURES

When environmentalists accuse BP of being split between two motives, they are correct. BP's environmental and social programs *are* equally driven by moral conviction and the desire for profit. This is precisely why they have become so successful. "Being green and progressive is not a separate attribute from the other things that we do but is embedded in the way we run our business. Our social and environmental programs allow us to outperform the competition in the short, medium, and longer term," confirms Browne.

The folks at BP approach social and environmental initiatives as if they were products, services, or any other critical stream of business. So rather than simply channeling company resources toward philanthropy, BP designs its most prominent social and environmental initiatives around a specific business purpose. "We understand that we cannot be all things to all people," Browne says. After identifying an unmet need, BP determines the viability and potential worth of its green solutions:

"As a sustainable leader, we choose a pace of development that retains a lead, and we determine the business value that this provides, while not moving too far ahead of the industry, thus losing connectivity and simply becoming the exception."

At least compared to the rest of the industry, BP certainly has become the exception, since it continually demonstrates the value of improving its practices by choice rather than by force of regulation. Browne believes that for natural resource–dependent industries in particular, positive ethical change should be more a matter of strategy than compliance: "This issue has to be seen in the broader context within which we are all running our businesses. Self-regulation has been gathering steam for some time, especially for safety and environmental issues, and particularly in Europe. There is an increasing recognition of the limitations of compliance and regulation as the tool to manage these issues," says Browne.

> "We demonstrate leadership by articulating what needs to be done, and by presenting the options that may exist for meeting those needs. In creating these expectations, we gain broader competitive advantage — with enhanced access to markets and returns."
>
> — Lord John Browne

"Unfortunately, there were, and remain, those who believe that the only way a company's environmental performance can be improved is by mandated compliance. Our experience proves that this is not the case."

A voluntary approach to regulation has served BP in multiple ways. In addition to diminishing the high cost of compliance and lowering other operating expenses, it has also given them a real competitive advantage. For instance, BP's emissions guidelines exceeded Kyoto protocol standards well before other oil and manufacturing companies even agreed to comply with them. The company implemented an open reporting policy in advance of the accounting scandals that rocked the American and international business world during the last few years. Its clean-fuel solutions were launched prior to any legislative requirements on fuel quality.

Guiding each social and environmental initiative is a company-wide policy of "no accidents, no harm to people, and no damage to the environment," combined with a rigorous, strategic methodology, including four incremental stages, each of which the company has managed to reach relatively quickly.

Stage 1, which occurred before 1997, focused on compliance. The resulting defensive initiatives produced during this

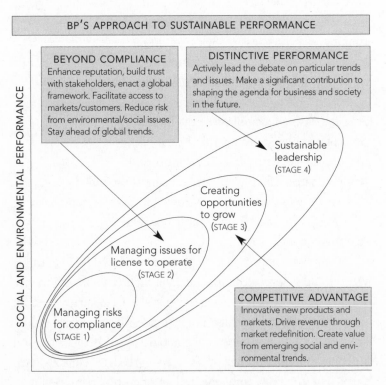

BP'S APPROACH TO SUSTAINABLE PERFORMANCE

SOCIAL AND ENVIRONMENTAL PERFORMANCE

BEYOND COMPLIANCE
Enhance reputation, build trust with stakeholders, enact a global framework. Facilitate access to markets/customers. Reduce risk from environmental/social issues. Stay ahead of global trends.

DISTINCTIVE PERFORMANCE
Actively lead the debate on particular trends and issues. Make a significant contribution to shaping the agenda for business and society in the future.

Sustainable leadership (STAGE 4)

Creating opportunities to grow (STAGE 3)

Managing issues for license to operate (STAGE 2)

Managing risks for compliance (STAGE 1)

COMPETITIVE ADVANTAGE
Innovative new products and markets. Drive revenue through market redefinition. Create value from emerging social and environmental trends.

ECONOMIC PERFORMANCE

stage were motivated mostly by regulation. This is where many companies find themselves today. But BP has managed to move into more strategically offensive territory. After achieving compliance, BP aimed to manage complex operating issues, to leverage competitive opportunities, and finally, to retain a leadership position in business sustainability.

With its current focus on sustainable leadership, BP committed itself to a continual process of innovation. It managed both to prescribe and to adapt future industry practices today and to do so without hurting short-term profits. BP continually launches programs that demonstrate how a positive link between social, environmental, and economic progress can work.

BP'S BEST PRACTICES

Following its sustainable leadership strategy, BP has implemented a vast range of successful initiatives falling into one of four categories: responsible operations, thriving communities, sustainable mobility, and climate change.

Most striking is the fact that, in addition to serving a greater purpose, each initiative essentially pays for itself. For instance, BP's open reporting policy promotes responsible corporate behavior and reduces the high cost of compliance. The company's House of Peace and Justice program supports human rights and limits potential business risks associated with the security of its workers and facilities in foreign countries. The BP Ultimate line of low-emission fuels improves air quality while gathering market attention and producing immediate revenues. And the company's energy use policy limits greenhouse gas emissions and reduces costs.

A CROSS-SECTION OF BP'S SOCIAL AND ENVIRONMENTAL PRACTICES	
RESPONSIBLE OPERATIONS	• Open reporting policy enables transparency of workforce safety records, business policies, operational procedures, and financial records. • Facilitation payments policy inhibits BP from paying, soliciting, or accepting bribes in any form. • Stakeholder engagement and location reporting programs manage social, economic, and environmental impacts of BP's operations in foreign countries.
THRIVING COMMUNITIES	• House of Peace and Justice program engages with foreign governments to proactively resolve tensions or disputes and to protect the human rights of local communities affected by BP's operations. • Government Partnership program converts oil and gas resources into billions in annual revenue—stimulating the economic and the social development of nations. • Social Investment program addresses urgent needs of communities in which BP operates, improving local infrastructure and increasing economic opportunity.
SUSTAINABLE MOBILITY	• New "BP Ultimate" product line provides better-performing, less-polluting gasoline and diesel alternatives in the U.S., the U.K., and Greece. • Clean Cities program delivers an array of unleaded, low- and zero-sulfur fuels in 110 cities worldwide. • System City initiative introduces more environmentally friendly and efficient lubricant and fuel packages for bus fleets.
CLIMATE CHANGE	• Energy-use policy saves fuel and enables ongoing reductions in company's greenhouse gas emissions. • Global Emissions Trading System reduces the costs related to lowering company emissions. • Natural gas development and promotion initiative seeks to replace oil and coal, thus lowering global CO_2 emissions. • Investment in solar, wind, and hydrogen fuel cell technologies drives the shift to renewable resources.

The programs cited in the above table reflect only a limited range of the company's total social and environmental activities. As part of its sustainable leadership initiative, BP is in the process of piloting green projects in an array of countries, in hopes of finding success models that can be replicated company-wide and eventually industry-wide.

BP's latest project in Malaysia, for example, called MATRO (Membrane Application to Recover Olefins) has demonstrated its potential value by using innovative technologies that reduce the plant's CO_2 emissions by 30 percent, while recycling hydrocarbons back into the production process, thereby lowering materials costs for the company. Similarly, one of BP's successful projects in the Philippines has demonstrated that using solar technology to supply isolated villages with clean energy — thus allowing for local irrigation, drinking water, lighting, and education, while driving the company's renewables business — can be equally efficient and economically viable. BP also considers less-energy-savvy nations a key growth opportunity; its success in coal-dependent China has enabled the beginnings of a natural gas infrastructure for the country, while improving BP's bottom line.

THREE KEYS TO BP'S SUCCESS
1. A company-wide sense of ownership, mission, and aspiration.
2. A company-wide focus on achievable material targets.
3. A positive correlation between social and environmental responsibility and profitability.

Browne notes that the company's successful programs and ensuing green transformation have been made possible by three factors. The first is a shared sense of purpose: "Doing

something positive for the global environment generated enormous enthusiasm and creativity," he says.[22] The second is the
company's relentless focus on achievable results, since no initiative is launched before BP determines, with the help of those
responsible for the company's operations, how feasibly material targets can be met. The third key to BP's success has been
the company's ability to cement the connection between
responsibility and profitability: "We have found that an action
focused on any one of the three measures of economic, social,
or environmental performance has positive benefits on the
other two. So it's not a matter of choice between economic or
environmental and social performance," says Browne.

OPEN COMMUNICATION

BP's social and environmental programs are steps ahead of the
mainstream. They are strategically and operationally integrated, financially self-sustaining, and comprehensively monitored. The company also has demonstrated the value of
another missing link: effective communication. If stakeholders
do not understand the reasons for and nature of a company's
responsible efforts, then the company will be less able to win
affinity and maximize potential rewards. Therefore, BP has
implemented a comprehensive communications campaign
designed to clarify its positions and to increase the visibility of
its green activities. The company is working to break through
to elusive groups, including nongovernmental organizations
(NGOs), corporate and governmental partners, the press,
shareholders, and the wider public.

Rather than relying on "green-washing" and positive spin,

the company's current public relations crusade, targeted primarily at NGOs and the press, seeks to clarify its standpoint and to offset the potential for misunderstanding. Chris Mottershead, BP's distinguished adviser on energy and environmental matters, explains the campaign's crucial message: "Underlying some of the specific criticism against us is a more general belief that the world does not need to exploit any new hydrocarbon resources. We do not believe this is a reasonable position. Both oil and gas should be developed to fuel economic growth and social progress. Our position is that hydrocarbons can be produced without serious impacts on the climate or increasingly on local air quality if modern technology is used. We believe that the single most important lever in avoiding serious climate change is the growth of [natural] gas to displace coal."

With its emphasis on natural gas as the bridge to using renewable resources, BP has launched an integrated brand campaign to convince the public that its posture is both progressive and authentic. BP's new tagline, Beyond Petroleum, illustrates the company's vision. "It is meant to serve as a powerful signal that the future will be different, and that while oil will remain the transport fuel of choice for many decades, natural gas will have a growing role in fueling clean power generation, and still more lies beyond this," says Browne. "There is an increasing spectrum of energy sources, and as a company, we are committed to increasing this range, particularly as energy becomes cleaner and less carbon intensive."

> We can't do everything at once, but we can do something to address your concerns. We can show, year by year, that the products we supply contribute to a progressive improvement in air quality — without denying people the freedom of mobility.
>
> — From www.bp.com

A corresponding global advertising campaign further lever-ages this position through an open, honest approach to reveal-ing the company's ambitions and achievements. It centers on the paradox of consumer desires both for a cleaner environ-ment and for the modern efficiencies that energy provides. Each ad responds to the concerns of real people regarding cleaner fuels, foreign oil dependency, and the need for alterna-tive energy resources with a statement about the company's progress so far.

In addition, on their website, BP welcomes commentary and criticism. This campaign, viewable at www.bp.com, aims at revealing the hard truth. As Browne notes, winning every-one over is not the point. Rather, the emphasis is on instilling a greater sense of empathy. If stakeholders understand that evo-lution is necessary in the energy industry and that BP must change itself one small step at a time, then trust becomes more achievable.

GREEN GROWTH

There is absolutely no question that, through its green efforts, BP has become a much stronger company. If one removed the green aspect from BP, then the company's worth would be greatly reduced. Today green and BP are inseparable concepts. "BP is not about to diminish its focus on environmental, social, or economic performance. We would no longer be BP if we did," says Browne.

BP has successfully translated its core values into policies and actions that drive economic growth. Therefore, as opposed to other companies whose socially responsible efforts have been more recently implemented, barely communicated, and casually monitored, BP counts returns today. "These benefits range from increases in profitability and improved volumes in some markets to an ability to define our own schemes for reducing the impact of our operations, rather than having them prescribed by regulators," explains Browne. "There is also strong evidence that a green and progressive brand has allowed us to access the highest-quality staff — particularly young graduates."

> Good business is simply good business and will continue to deliver collective improvements to our financial, social, and environmental performance.
>
> — Lord John Browne

Recent figures reported by the company reflect clear financial and operational advantages. Today BP is far more efficient and robust than it was before its green efforts. To date, the company has

- increased revenues by $95 billion between 1998 and 2002;[23]

- achieved an annual solar business growth rate of 20 percent;

- reduced CO_2 emissions by 16.9 million tons since 1997;

- reduced total air emissions by 23 percent since 1999;

- saved $650 million in energy costs since 1997;

- reported 30 percent fewer oil and chemical spill incidents than in 1999;

- reported 94 percent fewer safety incidents than in 1987.

While these results are impressive in and of themselves, their collective impact is far more significant. As a corporate leader, Browne has a great deal riding on his shoulders because of the company's size. "Many people are dependent on our success," he notes. Last year, BP returned $5 billion to its shareholders and employed more than 115,000 people worldwide. It channeled $30 billion to 140,000 companies by procuring goods and services and returned another $48 billion in tax dollars to governments across the globe. In conjunction with its employees, the company also invested $97 million in community programs and charity organizations and contributed more than 108,000 hours of volunteer time.

Perhaps the most notable aspect of BP's influence lies within the energy industry itself, since the company's green actions have generated a macroeconomic tidal wave. BP predicted the rise of the renewables era and has positioned its resources and, as it turns out, the resources of others accordingly. Since Browne's 1997 declaration, the top energy companies in the world — including ExxonMobil, Royal Dutch/Shell, and Chevron Texaco — have invested millions in various processes intended to minimize waste and greenhouse gas emissions. Over the past five years, each of these companies has worked to instill stricter social policies regarding human rights and safety and to produce more transparent reporting of their social and environmental impacts. In addition, Shell has entered into the renewable energy market with considerable investments in solar and wind technologies. These other oil giants follow a greener path not simply because BP did it first, but because BP proved that it was worthwhile.

PEARLS OF WISDOM

Today Interface and BP are strikingly different companies than they were ten years ago. Anderson and Browne made conscious choices to transform their businesses from within, and both organizations experienced pronounced change. However, neither company was reborn overnight. What made these corporate transformations so successful was the way the change was implemented — gradually, tactically, and completely in line with shareholder interests. Another factor was strong moral leadership, which served as a foundation for positive results.

Browne and Anderson are beacons for corporate leaders who fear morally led change. To deny any company, no matter how large, the chance to become more socially and environmentally responsible based on a belief that such progress is too difficult, too expensive, or too risky is as irresponsible as it is ignorant. The idea that social and environmental performance must come at the expense of economic performance is an illusion. Only those who can see the strategic opportunities that exist beyond this illusion will be able to seize future benefits for their shareholders.

If Interface and BP prove anything, it is that integrity and courage can revive corporations. Although very different in style and approach, both Anderson and Browne embody these critical traits. Though neither holds a perfect track record, both are dedicated to improving their businesses and industries through responsible actions. Anderson encapsulates their shared perspective: "At the end of the day, the role of business is to generate prosperity and a better quality of life for everyone. So we should never operate at the expense of the earth or societies or future generations." Business success, it turns out, is not a zero-sum game.

WHAT ADVICE CAN YOU GIVE TO OTHERS WANTING TO TURN THEIR BUSINESSES AROUND?	
RAY ANDERSON	LORD JOHN BROWNE
"It is up to you to challenge the prevailing mind-set or paradigm that underlies the system. The current business mind-set is totally flawed, which is why most businesses are equally flawed. We must recognize that the earth's resources are not infinite and that all company actions have an impact on wider society and future generations. If enough of us acted with this understanding, then the world would change for the better. So before you make any business decision, ask yourself the question, What would the consequences be if everybody did it? Think big picture, and then change one step at a time."	"Simply do the right thing. As businesspeople, our key role is to create wealth both for shareholders and for the wider societies within which we operate. This can only be achieved by embedding a principle of 'no harm, no damage' throughout every aspect of business. Corporate responsibility is not an afterthought or a piece of public relations. Today's issues are too transparent for that. Ultimately, doing the right thing creates opportunities, builds trust, and creates commitment — all of which enable the collective improvement of a company's financial, social, and environmental performance."

CHAPTER TWO

ROOTING VALUES

Eziba • Stonyfield Farm

Perfection is achieved not when there is nothing more to add, but when there is nothing left to take away.

— Antoine de Saint-Exupéry

Steadfast ethics are not a peripheral consideration, but the foundation for a modern breed of business. Eziba and Stonyfield Farm are two companies that were originally created to reflect sets of social and environmental values. In practice, these values drive every aspect of their businesses — from revenue models to sourcing, product development, marketing, and management. Strong ethics led to the commercial success of both companies, indicating that high ideals can indeed produce tangible financial rewards.

While many companies have to work hard to better themselves, others appear to have been born with almost faultless traits. Few modern companies embody this notion more than Eziba, an Internet and catalog retailer of decorative art products that are made by poor people in developing countries. When founders Amber Chand and Dick Sabot sat down to write the business plan for Eziba, their goals extended far beyond making quick money. From the start, they set out to "change the world by hand" and in doing so to create prolonged shareholder value.[1] Since the company's launch in 1999, they have brightly succeeded in achieving both these goals.

Eziba was the first dot-com to put a vital social mission first and to yield profits at less than $30 million in revenue at the same time. While the company's accomplishments can be traced back to a number of factors, a considerable variable seems to be the chemistry at the core of the unusual relationship between cofounders Chand and Sabot. This chemistry has produced an equally rare approach to business.

Sabot and Chand are the ultimate yin-yang pair. Dick Sabot is a world-renowned economist whose pedigree includes tenures at Oxford, Yale, and Columbia. As an original founder of Tripod, he devised some of the more enterprising merger and acquisition strategies of the late twentieth century. Chand, on the other hand, is a soulful artist. She has served as the head of a progressive museum shop and as a founding member of the Spirit in Business World Institute. One rules by intellect, the other by intuition. One quotes Krugman and Stiglitz, and the other the Dalai Lama and Rumi. Yet these two share the desire to reduce the gap between the world's rich and poor. Both share a vision for a newer, wiser form of capitalism.

Chand and Sabot joined forces to found Eziba for the singular purpose of demonstrating that a positive link can be forged between doing good and doing well. In practice, Eziba sells gift products made by some of the world's most impoverished citizens. Each of these products tells a story about the plight of the individual who made it, about the culture and history it represents, and about the improved livelihood made possible by its sale. Sabot explains the company's aim: "We are positioned as a counterweight to the critics of globalization, as there are still those who believe that to be successful in business you must act purely out of self-interest and take advantage of those at the bottom of the economic pyramid."

> We are determined to have the greatest possible positive impact on poor people in poor countries — proving wrong those who said we couldn't do it.
>
> — Dick Sabot

In addition to putting the best interests of the company well before their own, Sabot and Chand make the betterment of society their highest corporate priority. What is most impressive about the pair is the way they have framed global social and economic problems and then identified — and seized — the business opportunities within those sets of problems.

In just four years, Chand and Sabot have built a profitable social enterprise whose impact will be felt for generations. Through its commitment to fair trade and global social responsibility, Eziba has lifted dozens of artisan communities within Rwanda, Botswana, Kenya, Afghanistan, Guatemala, and other regions above the poverty line during a period of fierce globalization debates. Its high-margin, second-generation business model has yielded triple-digit growth over a three-year period, despite declining performance in their category. Chand and

Sabot have also convinced high-profile venture capitalists and competitive companies, including Amazon.com, to back them with more than $50 million in working capital, even during challenging economic times.

Though still relatively small, today Eziba is recognized as one of the most progressive and socially responsible companies in the United States. *Success* magazine recently hailed CEO Sabot as "the Johnny Appleseed of the New Philanthropy,"[2] while *Forbes* and *Time* magazines both rate Eziba as among the "Best of the Web."[3] Forrester research has put the company in the high-performance retailer category, along with the likes of eBay, and the *New York Times, Lucky* magazine, and *Slate* magazine have all regarded Eziba as consumer favorites. Such remarkable accolades have recently led industry insiders to ask, *How did they accomplish so much so quickly?*

ROOTING VALUES

All companies have a defined set of business goals, and most have identified a set of core values. But few companies have actually developed business models that work in complete harmony with these values. When a company is fundamentally rooted in its core values — that is, when every action is guided by them — it leads to superior performance results on multiple levels.

Eziba's original business model was designed to reflect social values in a way that allowed the company to operate most successfully. Sabot and Chand predicted that by making the company's social values "mission critical," they could greatly enhance their competitive context — while having a larger than usual positive impact on the world. They avoided the typical pitfall of separating their philanthropic vision from their strategic approach and acted with the conviction that by improving the social and economic circumstances of the developing areas in which the company operated, Eziba had a better chance of succeeding. Thus, the goals of achieving monetary as well as social profit had become fundamentally intertwined. The company's financial prosperity became reliant on its ability to fulfill social missions, while the social impact Eziba made was furthered by its economic strength.

Eziba's innovative model has given way to some radical business initiatives designed to empower, not diminish, its vendor groups. Through ongoing marketing support, working capital, and a steady stream of demand, the company consciously develops entrepreneurial self-sufficiency among its artisan vendor community, 80 percent of whom are women in developing nations. Eziba found that in taking a hands-on approach to training vendors and nurturing their skills, its supply stream, overhead costs, and delivery windows are more likely to be met with consistency. "Our buyers and designers inform artisans about which elements of the design of their products work best, and which do not work so well. Despite their difficult economic circumstances, we have found these artisans to be remarkably reliable and responsive," remarks Sabot.

Despite the fact that it is a relatively new company, Eziba has already provided numerous examples of how its approach to vendor relationships has enhanced the strength of its business and the livelihood of artisan communities. A few years ago, for instance, Eziba began working with women in Rwanda — both Hutu and Tutsi. These women had been

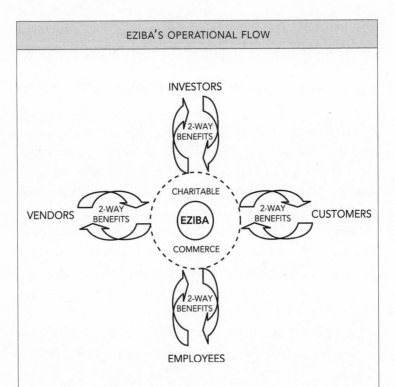

EZIBA'S OPERATIONAL FLOW

INVESTORS

2-WAY BENEFITS

VENDORS   2-WAY BENEFITS   CHARITABLE   EZIBA   2-WAY BENEFITS   CUSTOMERS

COMMERCE

2-WAY BENEFITS

EMPLOYEES

- Every facet of Eziba's operational program springs from the primary root value "charitable commerce."

- Every program the company engages in is designed to yield a double bottom line return (social and economic).

- The resulting social and economic returns also work as a two-way street, benefiting both the company and the participant groups. Participant groups benefit in the following ways:

> *Investors* get economic returns and the satisfaction that they have made an unusually positive contribution to people in impoverished countries.

> *Customers* get back precious pieces of culture and knowledge and the satisfaction that they have made an unusually positive contribution to people in impoverished countries.
>
> *Employees* get back generous incentives, meaningful work experiences, and the satisfaction that they have made an unusually positive contribution to people in impoverished countries.
>
> *Vendors* get back economic returns that translate into clothing, education, food, health care, the creation of jobs, a sense of empowerment, and the preservation of their craft traditions.
>
> - All the reciprocal benefits listed above have given Eziba the momentum it required to transition from a fledgling, well-intentioned start-up to a healthy and profitable model of conscious capitalism.

severely affected by the recent conflicts in the country, since their husbands had been lost in the genocide that ultimately claimed almost one million people in the struggling region. Instead of giving handouts, Eziba approached these widows with a business proposition. The idea was to use these women's intricate design and weaving skills to create hand-made Peace Baskets for the consumer market.

Like all Eziba products, the Peace Baskets tell a compelling story. For the widows, they symbolize reconciliation, economic viability, and hope for the future. For customers, they represent an effective way of reaching out and making a difference. And for Eziba, the baskets represent a definitive social stance as well as a consistent stream of income. The

Peace Baskets have succeeded on all fronts. Just a few months after the program's launch, Eziba had sold three thousand bas-kets — in effect lifting hundreds of women out of poverty and providing them with a new livelihood. "Their stan-dard of living has greatly improved as a consequence. Now they can afford to provide their children with health care and education," says Chand. Today Eziba's Peace Baskets are one of the company's best-selling items and have amounted to hundreds of thousands of dollars in gross revenue for the company.

> Eziba is based on the premise that entrepreneurial talent and energy is as abun-dant in most low-income communities as it is in Silicon Valley. All that is required to unleash that energy is the right environment.
>
> — Dick Sabot

More recently, Eziba has begun working with UNIFEM (United Nations Development Fund for Women) and other global agencies to replicate its Peace Basket model in strug-gling artisan communities throughout the world. A keen focus would remain on regions of conflict and postconflict, includ-ing Cambodia, Afghanistan, and countries throughout the Middle East. Chand reflects on the significance of the expand-ing initiative: "Without a marketing engine such as Eziba, these artisans would not have sufficient demand for their products. They would also be without the added investment to increase supply. Our program enables their products to reach a rapidly growing customer base, while the revenues generated directly feed the organizations that support their small busi-nesses [such as the Avega Widows Association in Rwanda]."

An intellectual property initiative is another side of Eziba's approach to vendor relationships. Since artisans from developing countries are limited by how much they can physi-cally produce with their hands, Eziba has created licensing agreements that protect the artist's original designs. This means that Eziba can now market high-quality art reproductions and turn greater volume, while artisans become capable of generating steady income without slaving away, since they receive royalties on the reproductions sold. Thus, a popular product generates substantial income for both sides. And by continuing to sell the original, Eziba also increases its value.

As Sabot explains, artisans require working capital to produce. When a company like Bloomingdale's places an order, it pays the vendor sixty to ninety days after the order is fulfilled. In contrast, when Eziba places an order with an artisan cooperative, it pays 50 percent of the order sixty to ninety days *before* the order is fulfilled. In other words, the company finances the production of the products it sells. "In effect, we have our own microfinance fund. We have borrowed millions from the Anodromeda Fund, a socially responsible European fund, which it relends, at no profit, back to artisans," he says.

By succeeding in its vendor programs, Eziba created new rules for American companies doing business in developing countries. The company's two-way model disproves the outdated assumption that the developing world represents little in the way of high-quality production abilities or economic opportunities. The model also negates the assumption that there is little demand among high-income consumers for products from these countries. Eziba's programs illustrate that a modern corporation can offer socially meaningful, internationally sourced goods that benefit supplier communities, while maintaining attractive profit margins at the same time.

> Our model is very practical, because businesses cannot succeed if their communities are failing.
>
> — Amber Chand

WHAT ARE EZIBA'S CORE VALUES?

Chand: Charitable commerce means an ongoing commitment to giving back. We choose to be a company that celebrates community service, and this has always been implicit in our operational model. As we began working with some of the poorest people on the planet, it became clear that our company could contribute to the well-being of literally thousands of communities around the world — not just economically but also culturally because we are working to preserve ancient traditions like weaving, embroidering, and ceramics.

Another profound value behind the company is collaboration. We have an absolute commitment to collaboration, whether with our artisans, our vendors, or our suppliers. We consider them partners. We take measures to ensure that our partners are feeling as successful as we are, so that the language and processes we use remain very democratic. When you think about what we're doing, we really are celebrating the world's most beautiful artifacts. We're celebrating this globally and internally within the company.

Sabot: I come at it from an economic perspective. It's been well understood by economists for a long time that companies generate costs and benefits that are not necessarily reflected in the company's balance sheet and income statement. These costs and benefits are called externalities. So, for example, intuitively we know that cigarette manufacturers' social costs are much greater than the cost of producing the cigarettes. These are called "negative externalities." GE releasing PCPs into the Hudson is another example of a negative externality.

On the positive side, there are likewise benefits that enterprises can produce that exceed the revenues they generate. I believe there is a social value to providing economic stimulus to poor people in poor countries, and that such social value transcends the revenue that Eziba generates. It is a "positive externality" to help reduce the gap between poor and rich countries. This is one core principal behind Eziba and other companies like us. We've internalized positive externalities and created a high-performance company in doing so. Internalizing externalities is more than hype and feel-good rhetoric. It has to be an analytical approach. You can't just talk about values, and all the while market something detrimental to society. To internalize externalities is quite a challenging thing to carry out.

TURNING VALUES INTO VALUE

Eziba's approach to improving the status of needy world regions has worked to generate vast social and economic benefits. In channeling more than $10 million back into artisan communities, the company has helped to reduce the gap between rich and poor nations, and developing communities have reaped an impressive range of benefits. In South Africa, Eziba boosted the income and quality of living for Zulu tribes people with AIDS. In Guatemala, the company's actions sustained ancient Mayan weaving traditions. In Kenya, Eziba saved irreplaceable tropical hardwood sources while supplementing the income of local farmers.

The company's charitable actions have also created business results ranging from supply-chain efficiency to new streams of income, increased employee morale, and a distinct competitive edge. With its rich presentation, everything Eziba sells is designed to inspire and inform the shopper about the story and the people behind the object. As a result the company has gained credibility over other retailers offering similar products with little or no humanitarian component. Eziba has been able to unleash a sort of private-sector activism that has worked to establish a strong, lasting bond with consumers.

Evidence of burgeoning customer loyalty lies within the company's rapidly expanding database of more than two hundred and fifty thousand unique names, which has flourished almost exclusively through vital word-of-mouth communication. In 2001 Eziba's exclusive database grew by a factor of seven, while its conversion rate — that is, the percentage of database members who become customers — doubled to just over 10 percent.

> In every way, we've become a high-performance company by behaving compassionately, pragmatically, and responsibly.
>
> — Dick Sabot

Eziba's strong social mission never came at the expense of its revenue model. During the company's first three years, revenues reached more than $10 million in annual sales, while the company managed to lower costs and sustain profit margins. While their revenue may seem like peanuts compared to that of larger-scale enterprises, it is a considerable accomplishment to have finished a full year ahead of the original financial plan. This is a rarity for any start-up, particularly a dot-com.[4] By the end of 2002, the company

- tripled revenue in a three-year period;
- reduced total expenditures by more than 40 percent in a two-year period;
- reduced the cost of customer acquisition to $3 per customer;
- increased the average yield per customer to $12;
- increased profit margins to an average of 65 percent;

- increased the size of key vendor incomes by 50 percent per year;
- forged strategic retailer partnerships, increasing distribution, by 15 percent.

Results like these have caused the financial community to take notice, while the company's original investors and founders have reemphasized their support to the social cause by devoting a portion of their stock to the Eziba Artisans' Trust — an initiative devoted to supporting the interests of artisans in developing countries. Going forward, Eziba pledges to remain dedicated to elevating global living and business standards and to demonstrating why solving the poverty problem makes good financial sense.

LEADING OUT LOUD

Foremost experts on corporate ethics have indicated that the most effective leaders tend to be quiet, flexible, and patient. These leaders pick their battles selectively, "bend vs. break the rules," and "put things off until tomorrow."[5] If this were really true, then the leadership approach of Gary Hirshberg, CEO of organic yogurt company Stonyfield Farm, might be considered ineffective. But evidence exists to the contrary.

Hirshberg is an idealistic corporate crusader, a straight-talking kind of guy who is not at all inclined to temper his personal convictions: "Historically, some of my employees have been aghast at my personal politics, but there have also been a lot of believers. My business approach of constantly challenging the system is working, even if people don't agree with every point I make. In fact, I would say that taking a personal stance on tough issues has been a key to Stonyfield's success."

In just twenty years, Hirshberg has managed to transform his social, political, and environmental views into a highly successful $150 million dairy empire. But despite Stonyfield's current status, the early steps taken by the company were about as modest as can be imagined. The company started with a great yogurt recipe, a sense of activism, and little else.

Much like a president who has served in the military, Hirshberg began his career in the trenches — milking the cows in a makeshift, gas lantern–lit farming school housed in a dilapidated New England barn. These were the obscure origins of the company that later came to be known as Stonyfield Farm. According to Hirshberg, since the five cows the fledging company did manage to own kept kicking over buckets of milk, he and his bright-eyed hippie business partner, Samuel Kayman, often had to milk day and night to keep the company afloat. Although undeniably character building, it is an experience that both men are glad to have left behind: "We were attempting to be a role model for treating the earth kindly while at the same time creating a great business — but, in fact, we were only succeeding as a model of how to burn out and die young."[6]

> We based the company on an assumption that consumers would be drawn to organic. We believed that they would 'vote at the checkout.' Twenty years later, our hypothesis has proved correct.
>
> — Gary Hirshberg

Like many eco-ventures, the Stonyfield concept did not take off immediately. Over time, Hirshberg and Kayman found that the key to breaking through was convincing powerful food retailers that organic yogurt was sellable. They had to prove themselves reliable, and their business more than a fleeting phenomenon. But instead of number crunching, Hirshberg pestered people to get his product into stores: "I put on my tie and jacket, drove to Boston, kicked the manure off my boots, and went to see Stop & Shop [the largest supermarket chain in New England]. They passed me from buyer to buyer until one of them finally gave me five stores — five very difficult stores — just to get rid of me."7

Since winning its first major account, Stonyfield has grown into the fourth-largest yogurt brand in the United States. The company is now a vital part of the multibillion-dollar French conglomerate Groupe Danone. In 2001, Danone purchased 40 percent of Stonyfield's stock and significantly expanded its reach, bringing the organic yogurt brand to thirty countries across the globe. That makes Hirshberg one of the most success-ful and well-known organic entrepreneurs in the country. It also makes him one of the more enterprising: Owing to the terms of the agreement he struck with Danone in which employees are protected from layoffs, Hirshberg and Stonyfield management remain in charge of the product, and the company's steadfast ecological policies are left untainted.

SUSTAINING COMMUNITY, EARTH, AND BRAND

Stonyfield isn't just a company that sells yogurt. It also fosters optimism about the way food is used and produced, about the meaning of corporate activism, and about the future.8 Hope is the core value of the company, and through the bulk of its activities Stonyfield translates this value into winning busi-ness approaches that improve public health, increase farmer prosperity, and detract from global warming. "There is an absolute need for people, especially those within corporate America, to change their behavior for the better. As a company, we're at the center of a major paradigm shift, and every day, more customers, employees, and suppliers are interested in being part of our solutions," says Hirshberg.

Since its inception, Stonyfield has developed a range of programs that support its mission of delivering hope, while building competitive distinction for the brand. In stark contrast to most other food manufacturers, Stonyfield invests in the New England dairy farms that supply its ingredients. The company converts them into organic farms, improving their soil, water, and sanitary conditions. By making these investments, Stonyfield can depend on receiving higher-quality ingredients, while supplier farms are able to command higher profit margins for the goods they supply.

Hirshberg notes the vitality of the company's farmer advocacy approach: "Our farmers are surviving at a time when lots of others are going under. Organic production is the only hope for New England's dairy farms right now." In addition to commanding higher prices, organic farmers experience the health-related benefits of a diminished reliance on hazardous chemicals. "They can hug their children at the end of a work day because they're not covered in toxic white dust, and they can swim in clean ponds and enjoy a life free of sprays and mounting health problems." Meanwhile, as demand surges, the manufacturing costs of organic go down, and both farmers and Stonyfield reap the rewards. "It's a virtuous loop," says Hirshberg.

To get a sense of how Stonyfield's farmer-advocacy programs

> Most of the agricultural industry is dedicated to screwing the farmer, whereas our mission is to channel more money to them. If you don't have families farming, you can't have healthy foods.
>
> — Gary Hirshberg

have affected the wider farming community, consider this fact: more than half of all dairy farms in New England are in Vermont, accounting for about 56 percent of the total milk production in the six states. In 2003 it was estimated that between 115 and 300 of those Vermont dairy farmers will go out of business, resulting in a net loss to the state of around $120 million.[9] Vermont's governer, Jim Douglas, recently characterized the crisis: "[The situation that] Vermont dairy farmers now find themselves in is very grave, and dairy price forecasts for the remainder of 2003 show little sign of improvement."[10] Hirshberg estimates that the conversion of farms to organic will help to offset the state's losses by adding another $80 million back into the economy.

In its category, Stonyfield has achieved a number of firsts. In addition to supporting farms, the company also works to improve the environment. Stonyfield does this by quantifying the value created by all its environmental and social activities. Hirshberg refers to the sum of these impacts as an "ecological footprint." Quarterly the company monitors the amount of CO_2, solid waste, and airborne emissions released during the manufacturing process. It also monitors total water and energy consumption, company-wide. "We take these measures to ensure that we continue to steadily reduce any negative impact on the planet," said Hirshberg.

The rigorous tracking of these "footprints" has led not only to saved resources but also to product and packaging innovations. For instance, in 2003 Stonyfield took the lids off its products, replacing them with a thin foil seal. And though this decision ultimately had little influence on consumers' purchasing behavior,

> Business is the most powerful force on the planet, and most environmental problems exist because business has not made the environment a priority.
>
> — Gary Hirshberg

it did have a dramatic impact on the company's ecological foot-print — reducing waste volume by more than 106 tons and using 16 percent less energy and 13 percent less water annually. The move also created a net savings of more than one million dollars.

In 2004, the company unveiled further packaging innova-tions. It now uses its reengineered foil lids as billboards that promote consumer education and activism. Along with the brand logo, the lids now contain health and environmental messages like "Cut the emissions. Sign the petition," "Choose fruits and vegetables that can lower your exposure to pesti-cides," and "We oppose artificial growth hormones." In addi-tion, the company recently began using a new "form, fill, and seal" machine, which, the company estimates, will lead to sub-stantive financial savings while preventing another five hun-dred thousand pounds of packaging from being produced every year. "Our ecological efforts have been very good for employee morale and consumer goodwill. And we can then reinvest saved dollars into marketing and growing the product line."

As Hirshberg attests, Stonyfield's unique business approach has created financial benefits and competitive distinction. How-ever, the company has not executed its programs without risk. For instance, investing in organic instead of chemically treated dairy has meant a higher cost of goods sold. As a relatively small food company, Stonyfield also lacks the manufacturing efficien-cies of larger companies like General Mills, so its process costs are relatively high. Hirshberg justifies the company's policies: "Although our cost of production is higher than the competi-tion's, our below-the-line marketing budget is far smaller." Since its launch in 1983, the company has held to its convictions, deducing that a socially responsible, eco-friendly approach would eventually enable the brand to attain what Hirshberg describes as the "holy grail" — that is, fierce customer loyalty.

STONYFIELD'S ECOLOGICAL FOOTPRINT: PROGRAM RESULTS FOR 2002	
SOLID WASTE REDUCTION PROGRAM	• Reduced energy consumption by 16 percent — enough to power 108 U.S. households for a year • Reduced water consumption by 13 percent — amounting to 800,000 gallons • Created a net savings of 106 net tons of solid waste material per year • Saved company resources
SOURCE WASTE REDUCTION PROGRAM	• Reduced waste volume by more than 10 million pounds; avoided 6,000 metric tons of CO_2 emissions • Donated more than 2 million pounds of yogurt to food banks • Diverted more than 5 million pounds of "waste" food — producing over 75,000 pounds of feed for organic pork • Saved company resources
ENERGY CONSERVATION AND MITIGATION PROGRAM	• Offset 100 percent of the company's CO_2 emissions through global ecological initiatives • Mitigated more than 20,000 metric tons of global warming gasses • Saved more than 24 million kWh of electricity — reducing an additional 7,500 tons of CO_2 emissions • Saved company resources
ORGANIC FARMING PROGRAM	• Supported more than 20,000 acres of organic farmlands, eliminating the use of more than over 100,000 pounds of pesticides • Supported more than 35,000 acres of Brazilian sugar lands — saving various wildlife species • Used more than 150 million pounds of organic ingredients • Saved hundreds of U.S. family farms through organic conversions

Today Stonyfield continues to convert more customers to organic yogurt and to win market share faster than nearly any other company in its class. Hirshberg explains why: "The positive word-of-mouth created by our socially responsible actions has driven interest in the brand and kept our customers coming back." According to the company's supermarket partners, when Stonyfield is out of stock, customers frequently complain to store management, whereas when competitive brands run out, customers tend to switch brands.

> We've blown right past Columbo, who used to be a far larger brand than us. By showing consumers that they could shop responsibly without too much hassle, we created brand allies.
>
> — Gary Hirshberg

ORGANIC GROWTH

Like its yogurt, the company's financial success has evolved naturally, without the added push of marketing ploys. "Over the years, our reputation as a conscious, healthy, and friendly brand has won us new customers. Our research shows that those customers tend to stick with us over the long term," Hirshberg says.

SELECT CUSTOMER FEEDBACK FROM 2002

"Stonyfield is my favorite brand [of yogurt], even though they are the most expensive."

"I have never actually gone out of my way to recommend a food product, but *this* yogurt I have."

"Stonyfield Farm yogurt is most appealing since it gives me something natural, good tasting, and a company I feel I can trust."

Whether or not you agree with Hirshberg's economics, politics, or idealistic schemes, it is beyond dispute that his socially conscious business strategies have worked and that they have benefited the company and its customers, the farming community, and the environment. In addition, Stonyfield has demonstrated superior quarter-after-quarter returns on every economic indicator.

With the investments made by Groupe Danone, Stonyfield Farm is now the largest organic yogurt brand in the world. The company retains a 40 percent share of yogurt in the natural food channel in the United States, which is a larger volume than the next five organic brands combined. They are by far the fastest-growing yogurt brand in supermarkets, growing at a pace double the average of the rest of the category.

Stonyfield has decided to amplify its advertising efforts for 2004. But instead of tooting its own socially conscious horn the way so many other companies do as part of their all-too-familiar "green-washing" campaigns, Stonyfield will place ads that will simply remain focused on the product's fundamental good nature — yet another sign that the new social responsibility is more than skin-deep.

WHAT FACTORS HAVE PLAYED THE BIGGEST ROLE IN CREATING YOUR SUCCESS?

Hirshberg: There are several, the first of which is quality. By investing more in our manufacturing process, we end up with a superior product in terms of taste and health benefits. Consumers agree that organic tastes better, and over the years they are becoming more aware of the related advantages. Many people who are dealing with health issues end up eating Stonyfield products because we provide inulin [a plant-derived supplement that stimulates the growth of beneficial intestinal bacteria], six cultures, and all kinds of other helpful elements as a result of our ecological policies. This creates a powerful bonding effect.

The second factor is activism. Consumers are worried and looking for solutions to environmental and health problems. They want to be able to trust and purchase from a company that is doing the right thing along these lines — so we spend a lot of time interacting with them about what we're doing and why. We help them grow more conscious of the *real* costs of nonhealthy foods and more aware of the healthier options available. There's far too much blind faith in chemical applications in this society. Our corporate strategy, along both health and environmental activist lines, has been quite a conscious one. We've engaged in ongoing conversations with our public as a way to educate them about solutions and put their minds at ease. And it's a wonderful coincidence that our activism has been a key part of the winning business formula.

Also, you can't produce a superior product without a great workforce, so we had to make believers out of the people who work here. This is easy to say but harder to do. We have many employees who have come over from Columbo, which is now owned by General Mills. These people have become fellow missionaries. They don't use the same language as I, and they are not quite as strident about the mandate and absolute need for humans to change their behavior, but they have seen the power of the strategy. They believe in the company.

The fourth factor is supplier loyalty. Our farmers are surviving at a time when lots of other, nonorganic farmers are going under. We have more loyal suppliers and lasting relationships because costs keep going down over time as organic production increases. This is saving Stonyfield tons of money.

My advice to other business leaders and entrepreneurs reading this is never to underestimate the power of doing good. It's the most powerful force out there. What goes around does come around, so companies must begin to more carefully scrutinize the wider social and environmental effects of their actions. Our investment in doing good has endeared us to consumers. Some hate us, but the ones that don't are fiercely loyal and tell others, and so on. Right action creates a stream of positive side effects, including tangible financial rewards.

THE PURSUIT OF PERFECTION

The Eziba and Stonyfield stories demonstrate that it is possible to integrate socially responsible values into every aspect of a company's dealings, from the product itself to manufacturing methods, sourcing policies, and delivery systems. These stories also demonstrate the importance of cultivating a company's ethical business policies over time — stretching into new, previously uncharted territory.

Both Eziba and Stonyfield are engaged in a continual process of self-improvement, as Hirshberg indicates: "There are many areas where we are not where we want to be. We have become a zero-emission company for the last five years in terms of our manufacturing and processing, but we still produce carbon, so we invest in tree planting and converting diesel buses to natural gas and many other things to offset the production of carbon. And we haven't even begun to measure the carbon that comes out of our shipping and our employees' commuting miles. We still have a long way to go." He adds: "It's important to be candid in disclosing what our results are and aren't. This is a part of what being ethical means."

Chand and Sabot agree that continually analyzing emerging situations is critical to ethical performance: "Different economic, political, and legal events often give rise to newer forms of governance. Constantly managing the relationships that arise between buyers and sellers — between high-income countries and sellers from lower-income countries, for instance — is particularly important," says Sabot.

When a company knows what it really stands for, and when this knowledge guides company decisions about what to do and what not to do in *every* situation, then the problem of ethical compliance largely fades away. Owing to their wholehearted approach to ethics, these companies are steps ahead of competitors in their categories. They develop their ethical policies proactively and tactically — leaving no stone unturned in the quest for superior, value-led performance. Their extraordinary achievements reveal why ethics are better approached as a journey, not a destination.

HOW DO YOU DEFINE ETHICS?		
DICK SABOT	AMBER CHAND	GARY HIRSHBERG
"Ethics don't come from the heavens, in some abstract form. They are rules that evolve in particular situations. Rules that all parties agree to abide by fundamentally because they work. When there is an unequal balance of power in business relationships, ethics come into play because they can offset that bias of power."	"Ethics go beyond morality. They come from an inner awareness of what is right and what is wrong. They require a profound commitment to one's own authenticity. They are the pulse of what makes us breathe and drive how we present ourselves to the world."	"Ethics means leaving no stones unturned in an effort to reduce one's negative impact. You can only say you're attempting to be ethical if you're continually improving processes. You're not even in the game if you are consciously leaving whole areas of your endeavor uninspected."

CHAPTER THREE

COOPERATING

Avon • Timberland

Each time a man stands up for an ideal, or acts to improve the lot of others, he sends a tiny ripple of hope [that can] sweep down the mightiest walls of resistance.

— Robert F. Kennedy

Through their far-reaching programs, Avon and Timberland demonstrate how companies can better themselves by improving the lot of others. Instead of relying on traditional cause-marketing techniques, both companies went steps further by linking a relevant social crusade with their core mission. Each developed an integrated cause partnership program that permeated multiple levels of the organization. The ripple effects of these partnerships rekindled each company's workforce, garnered brand distinction, and made enormous strides for the cause at hand.

Women are the primary target audience for almost every product marketed today. Though they constitute 51 percent of the U.S. population, women make between 80 and 90 percent of all household purchase decisions. For these reasons, countless companies seek to win their affections by supporting one of the causes closest to their hearts: breast cancer. Since the early 1990s, the pink ribbon symbol has become almost as ubiquitous as the American flag. Literally hundreds of corporations are vying to prove themselves as vigilant advocates of this critical women's health issue. And while many of these companies have done reasonably well by their efforts, none of them has had the same impact as Avon.

Avon, the $6.8 billion direct seller of women's beauty and related products, is the leading corporate supporter of breast cancer research, prevention, and education in the world. Together the company and the Avon Foundation have raised more than $300 million for the breast cancer cause in as few as ten years. Avon's Breast Cancer Crusade, which sets out to provide women with direct access to a range of education, screening services, care, and research, now operates in fifty countries across the globe. Not only are the company's 3.9 million sales representatives the world's largest force of breast cancer educators, but the Avon Foundation, which disburses the funds raised by the Avon Breast Cancer Crusade, is now the largest corporate women's foundation in existence.

> To understand our motivation to support breast cancer is to understand the philosophy and corporate culture of Avon.
>
> — Andrea Jung

Over the years, Avon's commitment to philanthropy and women's causes has resulted in an anthology of awards and recognitions. *Fortune* magazine regards Avon Products as one of its Most Admired

Corporations, while *Business Ethics* magazine consistently places the company high on its list of 100 Best Corporate Citizens. For its contributions to the breast cancer cause specifically, the Avon Foundation has been acknowledged by organizations including the National Breast Cancer Coalition, the American Cancer Society, and the Cancer Research Institute. Meanwhile, Andrea Jung, Avon's chairman and CEO, is recognized by *Crain's, Business Week,* and *Fortune* as one of today's most powerful and effective business leaders.

As the "company for women," Avon provides not just beauty-related products, but also a range of programs designed to offer women entrepreneurial opportunities for enhanced economic, physical, and emotional wellness. So for Avon the breast cancer cause is a perfect fit. As Jung told us, "it is perfectly logical and natural to be a force for change in the issues and activities that were most important to our sales representatives and customers."

> I am committed to eradicating this disease off the face of the earth. It would give me enormous personal satisfaction to know that Avon Products was the company that elevated finding the cure for breast cancer from a dream to a reality.
>
> — Andrea Jung

But to understand why Avon has grown so committed to the breast cancer cause over the years is also to understand the character and motivations of Andrea Jung herself. Jung has a personal interest in solving this problem: "Having lost my own grandmother to breast cancer, I feel as anyone does who has lost a loved one. The reality is that every three minutes, someone is diagnosed. That means that every three minutes, another mother, daughter, wife, sister, son, father, husband, grandchild, or friend has been affected somehow by breast cancer. And if you talk with any of them, you will learn just how committed they all are to finding a cure to this terrible disease."

Jung has a remarkable way of taking her work personally and of rising to every possible challenge. Though this inner fire clearly burns deep within her, she has attributed it to her family's work ethic. Jung's parents emigrated from China in the 1950s. Her mother, an avid pianist, was a chemical engineer. Her father is a professor of architecture at MIT, while her brother heads a software company in California. As a magna cum laude graduate of Princeton University and a former executive vice president at Neiman Marcus, Jung herself seems to have been born with the knack for achieving.

Her determined approach has worked to transform and elevate the company as well as the cause. Since taking the helm at Avon in 1999, Jung's contributions have resulted in a revived product line, a renewed marketing approach, and remarkably solid worldwide financial performance. As opposed to its comparatively less impressive state of affairs during the early 1990s, the company now ranks number eight among the world's top manufacturing firms according to *World Trade* magazine and is also considered the Best in Business by the *News Journal.*

Jung's leadership of the company's corporate citizenship approach (a company-wide effort that encompasses ethics, philanthropy, and social responsibility) has been equally vigorous. She has embraced the original values set forth by Avon founder David McConnell — trust, respect, belief, humility, and integrity — and amplified them. As she puts it, "against the churn and complexity of life, some things remain the same. They're the fundamentals — the basics we all learned from our parents and our very first teachers. And they don't change. They're too necessary, too elemental in their truth."[1] Jung, unlike other CEOs in her class, has transformed her beliefs into actions, relationships, and tangible results. She set her sights on the $300 million fundraising mark for the breast cancer cause shortly after taking her post as chairman and CEO and has managed to reach that goal within only a few years by strengthening the company's commitment to women and their families.

COOPERATING

As more companies reassess what it means to be socially responsible, more will realize the potential of new routes. Avon is clearly one such company. Like others supporting the breast cancer cause, Avon could have written a big check. They could have launched a special event, or created a more extensive cause-marketing campaign to call attention to the relationship. But instead, Avon decided to go several steps further.

Devoted to finding a cure for the disease, Avon linked the breast cancer cause with its core mission. Since 1992 Avon Products and the Avon Foundation have raised money and awareness through an array of products and programs, while accelerating scientific research and providing women with direct access to care through partnerships with grassroots and medical organizations all over the world. Because the alliance between Avon and the breast cancer cause is so extensive, in addition to the extraordinary results achieved, this relationship represents a new paradigm for corporate philanthropy. Today breast cancer represents a central feature of Avon's identity, while Avon is the company that consumers most associate with that cause.

As Jung explains, the association between Avon and breast cancer was born not by accident, but by design: "We wanted to find out exactly what issues were important to women so that we could focus our efforts on something that was meaningful to them. So we conducted an in-depth survey of women around the world — an exercise that continues to this day — and discovered that women are more similar than they are different. Their needs, desires, fears, and aspirations are parallel, no matter where they are in the world. And, not surprisingly, their own health and well-being were major concerns. When we asked what health issue they were most concerned about, the global response was breast cancer."

> For years, breast cancer has remained the number-one health care concern of most women. So Avon's level of commitment to the cause has remained very focused.
>
> — Andrea Jung

Buy-in from shareholders and employees was equally present from the start because the issue aligned with the company's charter. Jung elaborates: "The Avon Foundation's role is to establish strong relationships with numerous women's organizations to impact the community. For its parent, Avon Products, the focus is on bettering the lives of women. Both entities serve the same purpose, which is why there has been a remarkable willingness on the part of everyone in the company to remain so focused and committed. This commitment is company-wide and global. Everyone has always been on board with what we wanted to do."

In creating its Breast Cancer Crusade program, Avon chose to address not only the cause that is most on people's minds but also the group of women most in need. Because of limited income and insurance, underprivileged women are three times more likely to die from breast cancer, 41 percent more likely to be diagnosed at a late stage, and 44 percent less likely to receive treatment.[2] But despite this reality, relatively few philanthropies and cancer centers focus on serving them well. "What sets our program apart is that we focus on the medically underserved — including the poor, the elderly, minorities, and those without adequate health insurance," says Jung.

The program's strategy was also needs based: "Recognizing the complexity of the breast cancer problem, we further distinguished ourselves from other companies that fund research through a single institution or scientific investigator. Instead, we chose to support a virtual network of research, medical, social service, and community-based organizations, each of which is making a unique contribution," explains Jung.

Unlike other companies or foundations supporting breast cancer, Avon's Crusade concentrates on five critical areas: awareness, education, and advocacy; screening and diagnosis; treatment; support services; and scientific research. "We've implemented a sophisticated and comprehensive philanthropic approach that addresses every facet of the disease," explains Jung. Within each of these areas, the company has implemented multiple in-depth initiatives.

USING CORE STRENGTHS

The success of Avon's Crusade is largely due to the company's skillful use of its two greatest strengths: an intimate understanding of women and an unrivaled ability to build strong customer relationships. "The fact is that our sales representatives

AVON'S MULTIPRONGED BREAST CANCER CRUSADE	
AREA OF FOCUS	**INITIATIVES INCLUDED**
AWARENESS, EDUCATION, AND ADVOCACY	• Avon Walk for Breast Cancer series raises awareness and funds. • Avon Pink Ribbon product line raises awareness and funds. • Kiss Goodbye to Breast Cancer campaign and event series raises awareness and funds. • Avon supports ongoing breast cancer seminars, conferences, educational materials, and advocacy training programs through the National Breast Cancer Coalition Fund.
SCREENING AND DIAGNOSIS	• Avon-CDC Foundation Mobile Access Program enables mammography vans for screening in underprivileged communities. • Avon BeSmart program provides Avon employees on-site access to mammography services for a reduced fee. • Avon Fellowships in breast imaging awards grants to leading cancer centers. • Avon Foundation Breast Care Fund awards grants to grassroots organizations that provide access to screening and follow-up care for underserved women. • AVONCares program at Cancer Care provides financial assistance and psycho-social support services for underprivileged women diagnosed with cancer.
TREATMENT	• Avon supports a network of public hospitals providing treatment and care, including Boston Medical Center, Grady Memorial, Stroger/Cook County, and others. • Avon supports Look Good, Feel Better seminars to help women overcome the appearance-related effects of breast cancer treatment.

SUPPORT SERVICES	• *Rise Sister Rise*™ Breast Cancer Resource Committee supports African-American recovering patients — including a model group program for children of women with breast cancer. • Avon funds "Y-Me," a national breast cancer program that provides minority women with support and education, and links them to screening and care services.
SCIENTIFIC RESEARCH	• Avon Foundation–American Association for Cancer Research (AACR) Global Collaborative funds leading cancer center research programs. • Avon–National Cancer Institute Progress for Patients program awards grants to scientists for transitional research. (This is the largest public-private partnership in the history of the National Cancer Institute and the National Institutes of Health). • Avon supports nine leading cancer centers to conduct innovative research, develop new technologies, and back "Avon Scholars," a program that assists young minority and women scientists.

are the friends, relatives, and neighbors of our customers. We knew that we could rely on them to build a successful program," explains Jung. Each facet of the Breast Cancer Crusade is designed to build a strong bond with the individuals it has touched and therefore to create swift momentum both for the cause and the brand.

Since the Crusade's beginnings, Avon has sought to provide constituent communities with meaningful ways to get involved. For instance, the Pink Ribbon product line — which includes a selection of lipsticks, jewelry, and accessories — puts funds back into the Avon Foundation's breast cancer efforts, provides sales representatives and customers with a convenient and affordable way to participate, and creates an opportunity for dialog about breast cancer. Jung describes the collective sense of mission that Pink Ribbon products have inspired: "Everyone, sales representatives and customers, feels a sense of ownership. They know that they are playing a vital role in solving the problem."

> Avon's grassroots, one-on-one relationship approach created the perfect environment where a personal issue, such as health, could be effectively introduced. This enabled us to raise awareness where it was most needed.
>
> — Andrea Jung

Avon also takes steps to ensure that both employee and consumer groups retain their connection to the cause and brand over time. For instance, the company posts the percentage of revenues that each Pink Ribbon product returns to the cause on its website. Jung notes that the impact of this transparency "instills a sense of confidence. It's a very important piece of information that both customers and sales representatives appreciate knowing."

The company's focus on building strong bonds is evident throughout other aspects of the Crusade as well, including the Avon Walk for Breast Cancer series, which in 2003 engaged thousands of employee and customer participants through a welcoming emphasis on a noncompetitive spirit and group camaraderie. Each walk is structured for all fitness levels, and participants enjoy free products, educational materials, overnight accommodations, yoga classes, meals, massage, medical care, and entertainment at the event's "Wellness Village." But the real charge behind the Avon Walk for Breast Cancer series is the powerful group psychology it instills, since sadly, so many participants are personally affected by the disease.

CREATING VITAL PARTNERSHIPS

While the Crusade's awareness, advocacy, and education initiatives have done a great deal to engage the public, the Foundation's screening, diagnosis, treatment, and support-related efforts fill critical gaps in the system. This is because the Avon Foundation has structured the bulk of its comprehensive partnerships with major medical and grassroots organizations in an effort to reverse historical inequities. For instance, the Foundation targets areas that are underfunded as a result of low federal and private support — such as the investigation of higher frequency and mortality rates among minority individuals with breast cancer.

Likewise, the Foundation requires that the ten leading cancer centers it funds, including the Herbert Irving Comprehensive Cancer Center at Columbia-Presbyterian and Massachusetts General Hospital's Harvard Comprehensive Cancer Center, devote a portion of their financial gift to providing state-of-the-art care to medically underserved women. "We want to ensure that all women receive parity in medical care, regardless of their economic or social circumstances," says Jung. "In addition to delivering clinical care to medically underserved women, these leading cancer centers pursue breast cancer research across a wide spectrum of scientific topics, offering the best opportunities in the fight against the disease."

> The partnerships that the Avon Foundation has formed with medical and grassroots organizations are integral in helping us to fulfill our mission. They define our approach to philanthropy.
>
> — Andrea Jung

The Foundation's major partnerships also include an alliance with the National Cancer Institute (NCI). This alliance, which was established through an unprecedented $20 million gift and later formed the Avon-NCI "Progress for Patients" award program, emphasizes minority and other medically underserved patients and works to expand research in breast cancer by funding U.S. scientists involved in early-phase breast cancer clinical trials and other studies related to prevention, diagnosis, and treatment.

Since 1993 the Avon Foundation Breast Care Fund has supported more than six hundred nonprofit, community-based breast health programs across the country. In 2003 alone, the Foundation funded 134 such programs. It also nurtured relationships with the American Association for Cancer Research, the American College of Radiology Imaging Network, and the Centers for Disease Control and Prevention to run national and international programs that support breast cancer research and education among scientists and survivor advocates; fostered innovative new research and screening tools; and provided underserved women all over the world with free access to education, screening, diagnosis, and support services.

Recently, Jung traveled to Spain, Argentina, and Brazil to assist in donating state-of-the-art mammography equipment and breast cancer screening services to local communities. As with the other Crusade efforts she has been personally involved in, these experiences rekindled her commitment to provide women all over the world with a priceless service: "Whether it's a [mobile screening] truck or a center, it's whatever they need, wherever they need it,"3 she says. Such pronounced dedication is evidently shared by all involved in the Avon Foundation's Breast Cancer Crusade, creating the largest impact possible for the cause and for the growing number of people who are affected by the disease every year.

MAKING A DIFFERENCE

Avon's contributions to eradicating breast cancer have been exceptional. The net results have created a clear stream of benefits for the company, the cause, and the women addressed. Jung summarizes the Crusade's meaningful achievements: "We know firsthand that Avon's support of the breast cancer cause has made tangible and life-saving differences to thousands of women and their families. And there is no question that along with the tangible benefits of being a good corporate citizen, there are the intangibles."

According to the company, the most important of these intangibles is enhanced employee and sales representative morale, along with employee and sales representative retention. For Avon, these issues are particularly critical because of its direct-selling model, as Jung explains: "Our own research has shown that many of our associates have joined Avon specifically because of our work in the breast cancer arena. In addition, most sales representatives report feeling an enhanced sense of pride when they see the difference our breast cancer program has made over the past decade."

The Avon Foundation Breast Cancer Crusade resources, programs, and outreach efforts have also enabled measurable social impacts. So far Avon's Crusade has touched millions around the world by enabling

- 201,890,000 free educational flyers to be distributed in twenty-one countries;
- 6,421,380 clinical exams in 360 cities in Mexico;
- 1,300,000 women educated in Ukraine;

- 1,000,000 women reached through 51 medical projects in Hungary;

- 1,000,000 breast self-exam cards distributed in Germany;

- 56,000 medical exams in Guatemala;

- 36,000 free mammograms in Argentina;

- 7,000 signatures on a petition to increase government funding of breast cancer research in Canada;

- 6,000 breast cancer–trained doctors, nurses, and lay-people in Slovakia;

- 2,000 women's health volunteers in China;

- 2,000 educational sessions reaching 70,000 women in the Philippines;

- 1,120 free mammograms in Puerto Rico;

- 120 trained nurses and 140,000 women educated in Poland;

- 800 funded nonprofit health programs in the United States;

- 650 trained breast cancer advocates in the United States;

- 200 funded researchers in the U.S. — 55 percent of whom are women;

- 25 funded medical research, screening, diagnostic, and clinical care institutions in the United States.

These achievements are indicative of Avon's decision to define the scope, duration, and goals of its partnership with the breast cancer cause in such expansive terms. The priority of eliminating the disease prompted the Avon Foundation to create a rigorous and integrated approach, which in turn created a cycle of benefits that has had a significant impact both on company health and women's health.

The results cited above are far from static. They continue to evolve as Avon's programs gain momentum in the countries where they operate. According to Jung, the Avon Foundation Breast Cancer Crusade will continue for as long as there is a need. That is the beauty of the partnership. The Avon Foundation's fight against the disease will not end until breast cancer does, making an eventual exit strategy a far more exciting prospect for all parties involved.

> I have personally met many women who have shared with me how our program has made a difference in their lives. In some cases, because a mammogram identified an early-stage tumor, for example, our efforts have actually saved lives. That kind of feedback is incredibly gratifying.
>
> — Andrea Jung

HOW DO YOU DEFINE CORPORATE PHILANTHROPY?

Jung: I believe that corporations have to look past traditional corporate philanthropy and embrace the larger issue of what it means to be "corporately responsible." This is an issue that's becoming an increasingly important priority for all Fortune 500 companies and particularly for Avon as a company operating in more than one hundred and forty countries.

It was Avon's founder, David McConnell, who more than a century ago defined the very character of this company when he penned our founding principles. Among them is "to meet fully the obligations of corporate citizenship by contributing to the well-being of society and the environment in which it functions."

These are not just words on the page. They are fundamentals of Avon. They are why the Avon Foundation was established nearly fifty years ago. They are why our ten-year commitment to women's health and the breast cancer cause is as strong now as ever. They are why we "invest" in the communities where we do business by providing employment to our associates and earnings opportunities for millions of independent sales representatives. And why Avon reaches out, particularly to women, offering education and empowerment programs to help them better their lives and the lives of their families.

SERVING COMMUNITIES

Not unlike Avon, the Timberland Company is built on a long-standing set of values: humanity, humility, integrity, and excellence. But the rugged footwear, accessories, and outdoor wear retailer's eighty-five-year heritage was profoundly invigorated when Jeffrey Swartz, grandson of founder Nathan Swartz and son of former CEO Sidney Swartz, took over the family business in 1998. As the next generation, Swartz entered his post as president and CEO with a new style of leadership and a progressive agenda to boot.

Swartz sought to turn Timberland into a twenty-first-century model of social justice and an agent of positive change. "I have always believed in the power of the individual, that one voice can make a difference. And at the same time, I remain convinced that the responsibility to serve should not rest on the shoulders of the individual citizen alone. Corporate America must play a vital role in building and replenishing the communities it serves," he told us.

Rather than promoting 1990s-style capitalist ethics, Swartz used his newfound influence to inspire greater levels of community involvement among Timberland's stakeholder groups. Under his guidance, the company's employees and, eventually, its consumers would become more eager to volunteer in their communities, while the brand would grow to embody civic ideals. "Timberland is on this earth to make superior boots, shoes, clothing, and accessories — but that's not *all* we can do. We can create enhanced value. We can take a 'short-term impact, long-term solutions' approach to improving the conditions of the neighborhoods around us, and improve our business at the same time," Swartz says.

As the company's new tagline "Pull on your boots and make a difference" promotes, Swartz has anchored Timberland on the notion that in addition to being profitable, business can also be focused on activating higher levels of responsibility, engagement, partnership, and positive change.4 As the primary means of manifesting this ideal, Swartz linked Timberland with a compatible crusade. Except, instead of supporting a broad-based cause as Avon did, the bulk of Timberland's attentions have been focused on a potent national youth corps called City Year.

> I believe there are many opportunities for business executives to extend and expand nonprofit relationships beyond the needs of an immediate crisis and contribute to the long-term growth of a nation.
>
> — Jeffrey Swartz

With its edgy tagline "Young enough to want to change the world, old enough to do it," City Year's purpose is to involve youth in civic-service projects that make a profound difference both in urban and in rural communities across America. Founded in 1988 by Harvard Law School graduates Michael Brown and Alan Khazei, the organization engages its members through a catching sense of nationalism and team spirit — two traits conspicuously missing from the average American's life. Eventually, City Year hopes that the most commonly asked question posed to eighteen-year-olds across the country will be, "Where are you going to do your service this year?"[5]

A DAY IN THE LIFE OF A CITY YEAR VOLUNTEER

It's 8:15 on a foggy morning. You're standing in Cesar Chavez Plaza, in downtown San Jose. It's raining.

Maybe you're fresh out of college, where you got used to late nights and later mornings. Maybe you haven't been up before 9 A.M. since you dropped out of high school to work full-time. Maybe mornings don't faze you at all — but then you're from Texas, where the mornings were never this wet. *You could be any of these people. You could be in City Year.*

You could also be back in bed. Instead you're standing shoulder-to-shoulder with your ten teammates, going through the readiness check. "Boots and belt? Check." "Name tag? Check." "Heart...mind...soul?" The last three are harder to measure — and, in the course of your day, they're the ones you'll need most of all.

After a quick routine of calisthenics (you shouted so loud they must have heard you in L.A.), the plaza doesn't seem like such a bad place to be. You're briefed for the day ahead; then you're off on a bus to your service site. *From above, you think, it must be quite a sight: sixty-five uniformed corps members, in five tight teams, fanning out to make a difference across Silicon Valley.*

Some take their energy to nursing homes. Some run day camps for kids. Your job is to tutor and mentor a class of fourth and fifth graders at Erikson Elementary School in South San Jose. Last night you put together a lesson plan about life among the Ohlone Indians. On the way to school, you go over your materials, planning what you'll say to your kids.

As soon as you walk into class, the room echoes with your whispered name. Over by the window, a little boy is pointing and mouthing "City Year!" to his friends. The teacher just smiles, pretending not to notice. You find a quiet place in the corner to work on multiplication tables with one of your students. She comes to you proudly bearing a self-portrait she's made. You tell her how pretty she looks in the picture. She's in fourth grade, and she still doesn't know how to multiply two times four. *That's why you're there: first to notice the accomplishments, then to fill in the gaps.*

Over lunch, your team sits down with the principal. She's worried about a group of boys who roam the playground taunting peers and picking fights. You talk about the problem, then pair off each boy with a City Year mentor. Out on the yard, he plays a game of one-on-one hoops with his new mentor: you shout out encouragement, you challenge him to hustle, you soothe his temper when he starts to get angry. The game ends when he walks off with the ball. *"Be patient," you tell yourself. Making change takes time, and you're in for the long haul.*

At 2:30 school is over — but as a City Year Corps member, your day is not. A quick team meeting, and you're on the bus again, racing down the expressway to a trailer park in East San Jose. Rains have been heavy across Silicon Valley. The Guadalupe River is about to flood its banks, and your team has been deployed to help finish the sandbagging. At the project site, you gather to hear instructions from a Red Cross volunteer, then scatter to fill in gaps along the assembly line.

You find yourself toiling beside a volunteer from the company that sponsors your team. [The company] urges its employees to come out for City Year projects, so she took off an afternoon to serve. You spend the rest of the day working under a light drizzle, shoveling sand into canvas bags until your arms ache.

At 5:30 P.M. it's finally over. Your team leader taps you on the shoulder, and the ten of you circle up to review the day. Just before the huddle breaks up, you glance around at the faces of your teammates. They have worked hard, their boots are soaking, their white T-shirts are splattered with mud. *But it's impossible to mistake it: they look less tired than they did this morning.*

It's time to do a readiness check of your own. "Heart... mind... soul?" Check.

From www.cityyear.org

To Swartz, City Year embodied the right mix of elements. It had a similar passion, idealism, and vision as he did. More important, it had a willingness and an ability to act on this mix. Timberland and City Year seemed like ideal partners fifteen years ago when the teams were initially introduced to each other, and, according to Swartz, they still do. "This is a relationship between two like-minded organizations wanting to create lasting change in the views of people and the landscapes [across America]. Timberland has the power and the responsibility to effect positive and lasting change. And when you layer in an organization like City Year that shares that passion, what we can achieve together is limitless."

Indeed, what the two organizations have managed to achieve together since forging their relationship has exceeded the expectations of both parties and of the business community in general. The two have redefined the type of value that a public-private partnership can create. So far the Timberland–City Year alliance has produced a New Hampshire–based volunteer corps composed of forty-five hundred Timberland employees, business partners, and consumers, plus numerous City Year volunteers. Together, this team has provided more than two hundred and fifty thousand hours of volunteerism to needy communities both in New Hampshire and elsewhere across the country. Moreover, Timberland has become the official outfitter for City Year's national corps of 6,511 youth and alumni, while the two organizations have collaboratively developed initiatives — such as mentorship programs and a Path of Service volunteer model — that serve as practical examples of positively influencing the course of a company and, for that matter, of a nation.

Over the years, the results produced by the Timberland–City Year partnership have been so remarkable that the alliance has been the focus of several Harvard Business School case studies and of numerous academic and industry articles. It has also received acclaim from the likes of three U.S. presidents, including Bill Clinton, making it one of the most high-profile examples of how to successfully mesh operational and strategic resources to strengthen communities and to bolster both entities' long-term worth.

Today the Timberland–City Year partnership enables what Swartz describes as a "two-way explosion in creativity, productivity, and effectiveness." The benefits for both sides have been substantial, since each has found its true calling through the other. Hundreds of thousands of community members have been touched as well, since the partnership has resulted in millions of hours of civic service. "We simply could not engage purposefully in the community without City Year's guidance and expertise," Swartz says.

Since the partnership commenced, Timberland has grown into a model corporate citizen, having been repeatedly acknowledged for its innovative approach to community service by organizations such as *Fortune* magazine, Business for Social Responsibility, the Points of Light Foundation, Businesses Strengthening America, America's Promise, and the Committee to Encourage Corporate Philanthropy.

Similarly, City Year has achieved a prominent stature of its own, having recently been featured as a national service leader by the *Washington Post* and the *New York Times.* "We are working to demonstrate, advance, and improve the concept of national service as a means of building a stronger democracy. There is not another company around that understands this like Timberland. Their commitment to us has been integral to every aspect of our growth over the past fifteen years," says Khazei.

> In my experience, our decade-long partnership with City Year has brought me great purpose and focus as a for-profit business leader and as a private citizen.
>
> — Jeffrey Swartz

City Year and Timberland came together out of a shared philosophy that service builds communities and brings about social justice. Today they remain together out of an understanding that strengthened communities and heightened social justice can create stronger organizations. A closer look at how the relationship has developed over the years reveals how the two managed to break through traditional philanthropic barriers to chart a mutual strategic course, and just how fertile such a course can be.

AN ESCALATING EXCHANGE OF VALUE

The potential of the City Year–Timberland partnership was first recognized in a business meeting in 1989. Shortly after Timberland made an initial donation of fifty free pairs of work boots to outfit City Year's growing youth corps, senior management from the two organizations sat down together for an informal exchange of ideas. As the meeting unfolded, the similarities between the two organizations' values and methods became strikingly apparent. The organizations used parallel language to define their missions and value propositions. Both had similar long-term goals. And both relied on a level of grassroots participation to meet their organizational objectives.

Swartz recalls his initial revelation: "When Alan came by to say thanks for the boots, I said to him, 'You are doing the things with your life that I dream about doing with mine. You are out there actually saving lives. I am making boots, but I have always wanted to save lives. And he said, 'Let me show you how they can be related.'... His message was 'Through me it's going to be okay to do what you dream and dare. I will provide you with the vehicle for your beliefs.'"[6]

After that meeting, Timberland contributed $50,000 to sponsor a team of twelve youth corps members, who were outfitted head to toe in Timberland gear for a fall semester of community service cleaning up local parks, working with the elderly, mentoring schoolchildren, and clearing nature trails. The next summer, Timberland supported two additional service teams with an investment of $100,000.

Because City Year's objective was to move past the "check cashing" stage to establish closer relationships with its corporate sponsors, the organization eagerly invited Swartz and his

CITY YEAR'S SOCIAL MISSION
"Demonstrate, advance, and improve the concept and delivery of national service as a means of building a stronger democracy"
TIMBERLAND'S SOCIAL MISSION
"Prove that doing well and doing good are inextricably linked. Inspire others to join us as we pull on our boots and make a difference"
CITY YEAR'S DELIVERY APPROACH
• Mobilize people around vital community service projects • Establish key corporate relationships • Leverage leadership tools to benefit for-profit partners
TIMBERLAND'S DELIVERY APPROACH
• Develop company-wide employee service approach • Establish key not-for-profit partnerships • Strengthen not-for-profit partners through funding and strategic resources

team to a day of service at a local adolescent rehabilitation center in January 1992. This outing gave Timberland employees a chance to get to know the personalities involved in the City Year organization, to examine its approach more thoroughly, and to experience its value firsthand. Swartz fondly remembers the residual impression of the event: "We were truly inspired by City Year because the organization offered us an opportunity to build stronger teams. We realized that this was something we needed to integrate into our own business model."

Months later, Timberland announced a three-year $1 million dollar investment in the organization, making it the largest corporate contributor. Timberland was now City Year's primary private-sector partner, and as a token of the relationship, Timberland became the official outfitter of City Year. This move enabled City Year, with its thousands of budding national volunteers, to establish a cohesive visual style and "brand" presence, while Timberland gained further recognition as a philanthropic retailer of outdoor wear.

Soon thereafter the relationship took a more collaborative turn. Beyond simply exchanging goodwill, the two organizations began exchanging intellectual capital and human resources. City Year volunteers went to work at Timberland offices to help with aspects of the company's operations, while Timberland loaned a senior officer to City Year to amplify the organization's marketing efforts.

> This is not philanthropy. Not only is the City Year partnership affecting Timberland's ability to further change and better communities, but it is also strengthening our infrastructure.
>
> — Jeffrey Swartz

At the same time, Swartz, completely inspired by City Year's commitment to volunteerism, developed Timberland's now world-renowned Path of Service policy. This policy enables all Timberland employees to take forty hours of paid leave per year to perform community service. In addition, Timberland instituted an employee Service Sabbatical program, allowing employees to volunteer with the nonprofit organization of their choice for up to six months. The company also instituted a Community Enterprise division, whose purpose was to further the City Year partnership and to organize company-wide community service events.

With a significant portion of Timberland resources allocated to growing the Path of Service approach, the cooperational partnership between City Year and Timberland moved into high gear in 1995. Swartz became a member of City Year's National Board of Trustees and a national spokesperson for the organization, while Timberland announced a $5 million investment in City Year over the next five years.

In turn, City Year, with its innovative range of leadership development tools, began facilitating team-building and diversity exercises with Timberland's senior management. Doing these exercises proved to be an invaluable experience for all parties involved. Swartz recalls their impact: "The use of City Year's unique leadership tools helped us to set company strategy and employ more innovative volunteer events. Many companies pay thousands of dollars for the type of team-building skills that we have learned through these experiences."

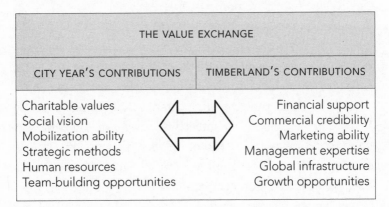

THE VALUE EXCHANGE	
CITY YEAR'S CONTRIBUTIONS	TIMBERLAND'S CONTRIBUTIONS
Charitable values	Financial support
Social vision	Commercial credibility
Mobilization ability	Marketing ability
Strategic methods	Management expertise
Human resources	Global infrastructure
Team-building opportunities	Growth opportunities

Between mid-1995 and 2002, Timberland and City Year would collaborate in a wide range of projects, including City Year Gear, a co-branded apparel and accessory line that enhanced the partnerships' visibility and channeled funds back to both entities; "Serv-a-palooza," an annual event at which volunteers rebuild, clean, and repair schools and community centers; and SkillsUSA-VICA, an ongoing program that promotes the development of leadership and occupational skills among various youth groups. At every step, Timberland remained focused on enhancing the business value of the partnership: "Our aim is to generate profits for City Year's operations and to employ their expertise to help solve our operational needs," comments Swartz.

In September 2003, Timberland and City Year increased the success of their fifteen-year alliance with the launch of the Community Builders Tour, a national event that unites local residents, community organizations, and select retailers for a day of community service in cities around the country. According to Swartz, "Community Builders Tour events are tailored to the individual needs of each community, and they serve to celebrate the power of collaboration, the power of service, and the power of community." In each city, service days close with a "service celebration" featuring live entertainment, new offerings from Timberland, and information about local community organizations. "Our mission with the Community Builders Tour is to build relationships and excitement around the ethic of service, and create lasting, positive change that will endure long after the tour has left town," notes Swartz.

To date, Timberland has made a $13 million financial investment in City Year. However, even for City Year, the value of the relationship extends beyond what money can buy. City Year and Timberland are now philosophically and operationally linked. Their values are integrated. They share their offices and human resources. Their strategic paths are reciprocal. As Swartz explains, the division between the two organizations continues to blur: "City Year leads our vision and diversity seminars and provides us with professional services.

In addition, they attend Timberland's sales and shareholder meetings, give presentations on the program to our worldwide employees and business partners, enjoy Timberland social events, and, in the form of alumni, they have even joined our staff."

As Swartz notes, this combined infrastructure was not an unplanned result, but an intended and encouraged goal. The strengths of each organization have nourished both, leading to what Swartz describes as "a better working unit and a far more satisfying workplace." Nevertheless, as Swartz also indicates, the strength of the relationship and commitment of both entities has been tested more than once.

GROWING THROUGH CHALLENGES

Since 1995 both Timberland and City Year have experienced financial difficulties that left many industry insiders wondering whether or not the relationship would (or should) survive. In 1995 Timberland sales declined, while operational costs increased owing to rapid growth in previous years. And as a result of difficult financial performance, the company had to close down two of its manufacturing plants and to lay off numerous workers from its New Hampshire–based headquarters.

These moves startled employees, and some became frustrated by the company's continued support of City Year programs. Elise Klysa, senior manager of Community Enterprise Programs at Timberland, recalled how the financial difficulties influenced employee sentiments: "When people are seeing their buddies laid off, and they know that City Year is getting a million dollars, they see that as jobs. It created a negative backlash that had to be managed very carefully. Where before the focus was on high visibility for City Year and integration everywhere, there were people that didn't want to see them at all. There was a lot of resentment."7

Instead of backing down, Timberland chose to deal with employee resistance head-on by strengthening instead of diminishing its commitment to philan-thropy. The company designed a series of mandatory service employee events to lift morale, to communicate a steadfast commitment to core values, and to cre-ate a positive social contribution. Swartz recalls their influence: "These events truly helped bring employees together during a time of crisis. Our social enter-prise division went on the offensive and promoted the Path of Service as an outlet for employees to step out of their work environments and just feel good about mak-ing some difference in their communities."

> We made it clear that our commitment to social responsibility, and by extension, City Year, was a core value of the company and therefore not subject to cuts.
>
> — Jeffrey Swartz

Although the company did have to buckle down to deal with the budgetary constraints created by financial challenges in the shorter term, its continued dedication to the Path of Ser-vice has ultimately worked to push the company through a rocky phase and to reach a series of impressive triumphs. Today Timberland's financial performance is up, while its ser-vice approach is a principal feature of the company's brand identity.

For City Year, however, the major obstacles have been beyond the organization's immediate control and therefore more difficult to overcome. In addition to private-sector sup-port, City Year relies on federal funding to keep it afloat. Ever since a Republican majority seized control of Congress in 1994, funding to AmeriCorps — a core element of President Clinton's national service legislation that works to support City Year and a network of similar organizations — has been at risk.

In 1995 Republicans proposed to eliminate the AmeriCorps altogether. More recently, a 55 percent funding cut was passed — effectively diminishing City Year's AmeriCorps slots from 1,110 to 551 in 2002. However, as Khazei conveys, Congress is currently poised to pass $444 million for AmeriCorps next year: "If Congress does pass this bill, we will have gone from the biggest cut in AmeriCorps history to the largest increase in funding in a single year. This does not guarantee an increase in funding to City Year, but it is a hopeful sign for the national service field."

Though City Year could not have achieved its national presence without the support of AmeriCorps, the funding crisis has highlighted the fundamental importance of private-sector partnerships. Since the crisis, Timberland has boosted its financial support of the organization. "It is because of companies like Timberland that City Year has been able to continue through this year with diminished federal support without closing any sites or cutting back on our infrastructure," Khazei says.

Khazei also indicates that the organization is working closely with its private-sector partners — which, in addition to Timberland, include Cisco Systems and Comcast — to refine goals and strategies and ultimately to improve mutual results. The organization hopes to provide a meaningful method for the corporate world. That is, according to Khazei, "a benchmark for best practices and high impact models in the community."

Along these lines, Timberland and City Year are currently working together to develop a community service–based leadership development program and a standardized model for launching successful community service events. Their mutual hope is that these tools will sharpen the partnership and enable other companies and nonprofits to replicate the success of their union.

WHAT ARE THE KEYS TO BUILDING A SUCCESSFUL COMMUNITY PARTNERSHIP?

Swartz: Fundamentally, a successful partnership requires both the business and the nonprofit organization to believe the joint effort is a win-win. It must have a mutually beneficial, strong relationship as its core, shared values as its foundation, and a shared vision for its future. This must be about more than the nonprofit receiving a check and about more than the business polishing its image.

The Timberland–City Year partnership is rooted in shared values and a shared vision, and it's also vital that the relationship between the company and the organization is marked by depth and breadth. A successful partnership cannot be compartmentalized so that only the CEOs speak to each other or the marketing departments communicate with each other; it must take root in all areas and be full service.

There are infinite examples of how extensive the relationship between City Year and Timberland is, including joining together for international service projects, Timberland sponsorship of events at City Year's convention, working together on uniforms, uniting for Timberland employees' community service initiatives, sharing leadership tools, and exchanging information about business processes.

The extent of the commitment to values, vision, and implementation of the partnership will determine the nature of the partnership. For City Year and Timberland, the relationship is marked by growth over time. It has strengthened and intensified since its inception. This is a hallmark of a strategic partnership because it indicates the level of value the entities offer one another. A successful partnership is not marked by a scattershot approach or occasional connections; it is instead furthering goals through a shared and ongoing effort.

Finally, the partnership must be marked by honesty, including the ability to share with one another internal needs or challenges. The open exchange of information is an important component of building a strong relationship because it is part of establishing trust between the partners.

Corporations and nonprofits have a lot to teach one another, and when they engage in this successfully, as with the Timberland–City Year partnership, each entity and the community benefit.

MUTUAL REWARDS

The relationship between Timberland and City Year has created compelling results on a social level: throughout hundreds of communities across America, neighborhoods have been cleaned, new parks and playgrounds have been built, and hundreds of elderly citizens and thousands of children have been served. In addition, through ongoing service and continued interaction with the Timberland team, City Year's youth corps has grown ever more committed to "redefining what it means to be young in America, and challenging who we consider heroes."[8]

From City Year's perspective, Timberland's ongoing investment has enabled the organization to greatly increase its impact and overall efficiency. "The people at Timberland were integral to our effort to build a national coalition of AmeriCorps programs, offering us advice and assistance every step of the way," says Khazei.

Thus far, the organization has managed to achieve healthy growth and to fulfill its mission of bringing about major changes in society while becoming a model for national service. To date, City Year counts the following achievements:

- Approximately one thousand corps members annually
- 6,511 alumni members
- 9.7 million hours of community service
- One international and fourteen nationwide service locations
- 686,641 served children through tutoring, mentoring, and after-school programs

Inversely, City Year's influence on Timberland has also created a stream of benefits for the company and its financial and competitive standing. The most significant of these contributions is the Path of Service approach, which, according to Swartz, has raised levels of brand distinction, customer loyalty, employee satisfaction, and publicity: "Employees tell us that our commitment to community was the deciding factor in their decision to join or stay with the company, and we remain encouraged by market data that suggests that consumers are more likely to remain loyal to socially conscious companies."

In line with its allegiance to community service, Timberland has recently

> While it may be difficult to prove that the City Year partnership directly raised our stock value, reduced our expenses, or increased employee productivity, we believe it to be true, and anecdotal evidence suggests that we're right.
>
> — Jeffrey Swartz

launched a new website: www.timberlandserve.com, dedicated to promoting civic values by informing, educating, and
inspiring consumers to get involved in their communities. This
site, in addition to the company's ongoing service approach
and partnership with City Year, ensures that the impact created by Swartz's focus on values will create a lasting legacy for
the company, future generations, and the corporate world.

BUSINESS AND COMMUNITY INVOLVEMENT

One would be hard-pressed today to find a corporate leader
who did not agree that serving the community is a good idea,
even a key ingredient to business success. Nevertheless, a dis-
crepancy between high-reaching corporate ideals and high-
impact community-based programs still remains. The Avon
and Timberland stories indicate that it is possible to create
integrated strategies that are as beneficial to the bottom line as
they are to the common good. Ultimately, Jung and Swartz
broke through the traditional barriers to social investment by
connecting these two fronts.

Timberland made the connection through a convergence of
interests, strategies, resources, and success measures, while
Avon achieved the link through a systematic, business-driven
approach to solving a critical social problem. But the two
approaches share many features. Both companies put a social
mission at the top of their business agenda and fulfill a set of
unmet needs. Both focus on what is unique about their way
of doing business and deploy social solutions accordingly. Both
harness the knowledge possessed by partnering organizations
to further the impact of the relationship. And both focus on

results. This combination of factors enabled each company to strike the balance between serving shareholders and serving society at large.

Perhaps the most remarkable parallel between Timberland and Avon is their underlying level of commitment to the cause. Swartz and Jung champion their initiatives with great personal dedication and enthusiasm. Intense belief in the importance of their respective crusades and a conviction that their company's efforts would make a difference served to convince others throughout their organizations. Such company-wide acceptance, in turn, helped facilitate the success of the partnerships.

Beyond their immediate worlds, Jung and Swartz acknowledge a need for more businesses to step up and play a vital role in their communities. They believe that civic engagement is a primary obligation of today's socially minded corporations, particularly given the pervasive and self-serving approaches so prevalent during the past decade. They also share the more persuasive conviction that actions that improve the well-being of communities by their nature also improve the shape of business, an outcome most of us want to see.

WHY SHOULD BUSINESSES SERVE THEIR COMMUNITIES?	
ANDREA JUNG	JEFFREY SWARTZ
"In an era when companies are expanding into more of the world's emerging markets, businesses are in a unique position to demonstrate their responsibility and commitment to the communities in which they operate. Giving back to the communities that have helped them become successful is simply the right thing to do. Good corporate reputations must be earned, and corporate community and social involvement helps companies to build good reputations that in turn help them grow and strive for continued success."	"Some believe that the only role of a company is to create value for shareholders. Some even hope that companies will 'not harm' their communities as they do business. I would say that the role of business is to create value for shareholders *and* to create stronger communities. Service to the community is a requirement. While companies should remain absolutely accountable to their shareholders, they must also accept and recognize their responsibility to work for the common good. Doing so can only make them stronger."

CHAPTER FOUR

TRADING FAIRLY

Green Mountain Coffee Roasters • The Body Shop

When you are right, you cannot be too radical.

— Dr. Martin Luther King Jr.

Standing up to corporate indifference and injustice is considered a risky move by many firms. Green Mountain Coffee Roasters and The Body Shop, however, reveal how the benefits of doing so can outweigh the potential risks. Through a vigilant dedication to fair trade, both companies set more equitable standards of commerce within their respective categories and created positive industry change. Their fair trade approaches also enabled them to grow more efficient and to gain significant competitive edge, while establishing a powerful new role for business in society.

Every day, Americans consume 324 million cups of coffee. Last year, the $55 billion U.S. coffee industry experienced record profit margins. However, most of the two hundred and fifty million people from around the world who depend on coffee for their livelihood are destitute, because only about 2 percent of them receive a fair price for their beans.[1]

These are facts that Green Mountain Coffee Roasters, a company known for its fair trade program, eagerly cites when framing its raison d'être. "There is no question that conditions for coffee growers are far worse than they were ten years ago. I recently visited coffee farmers in Mexico and Guatemala and was shocked at how much worse things have become," says Bob Stiller, president and CEO of Green Mountain. "Farmers are unable to support themselves. Families are being torn apart. Communities are being torn apart as busloads of men have to abandon their farms every week to look for more profitable work elsewhere." Stiller is describing just a few aspects of the social and economic devastation created by today's looming coffee crisis.

Chances are that the gourmet coffee in your cup came from a remote region somewhere in Central America, Mexico, Brazil, Colombia, or Vietnam. Since 70 percent of the world's coffee is grown by small farmers in those countries, it is likely that the beans used to make your coffee were harvested not by a large producer, but by a family farming four acres of land or less.[2] Many of these families have been harvesting coffee for generations, perfecting painstaking methods in order to present you with the best possible flavor. It takes anywhere from three to five years to harvest most coffee beans and a remarkable amount of labor, skill, and care to prepare them for sale. While your morning latte represents a little luxury to you, it represents an entire culture and economy to those who made it possible.

Today that culture and economy face total meltdown. Many of the once-lush coffee-growing regions around the world are desolate, and a significant portion of the population has resorted to crime, illicit crops, or illegal migration to survive. This is because the price of coffee has fallen dramatically in recent years — not so much the price you pay at the grocery store, but the price that many of the world's largest coffee companies pay to the farmers who supply their beans. This is also why the U.S. coffee industry experienced record profits last year.

The problem, Stiller explains, is that since the International Coffee Organization, the group that sets trade standards for the industry, collapsed in the late 1990s, production quotas have disappeared and floor prices for coffee have plummeted. Too many coffee companies have responded to the lapse in regulation by squeezing coffee farmers. In most cases, today's commodity coffee prices are below the cost of production, causing socioeconomic problems to surge and coffee quality to plunge.

> I saw desperation in the eyes of coffee farmers, and it was heartbreaking. Everywhere you turn in coffee-growing regions, there is extreme poverty.
>
> — Bob Stiller

It's a vicious circle that consumers are wising up to, and one that Stiller intends to continuously protest: "What many people don't know is that low-priced coffee comes at a devastating cost both to the supply chain and to wider communities. It is not sustainable. There has to be a greater transparency around how products are sourced. The consuming public needs to be more aware of the sustainability of many of the things they buy. Not just with coffee, but with other produce and products as well."

Conditions in the coffee industry are not unique. The word *coffee* could just as easily be replaced by the words *banana, blue jean,* or *soccer ball.* "Unfair trade," whereby companies profit by diminishing vendors to their weakest point, is an accepted custom that invades multiple spheres of business. For some of the largest corporations in particular, it has become the rule, not the exception. Green Mountain is on a mission to put an end to such practices — at least in its industry. The company proclaims: "With a worldwide oversupply of inferior coffee reducing the prices farmers receive, we have embraced fair trade to help stanch the crisis."[3]

Currently, fair trade is an international movement lead by nonprofits like TransFair, a fair trade certification organization. By working with corporations and supplier communities to establish floor prices and to streamline farming and business practices, TransFair helps build economic independence and empowerment in farmer communities around the world. So far TransFair's efforts, driven by the participation of ten thousand companies in the United States and thirty-five thousand companies in Europe, have enabled more than eight hundred thousand farmer families to achieve a better quality of life.[4]

> If there is to be world peace, we need to provide people with the ability to survive. We should be willing to pay a fair price for labor.
>
> — Bob Stiller

Since Stiller's initial trips to Mexico and Guatemala, his indignation over iniquitous corporate practices has peaked — and so has his devotion to fair trade. Green Mountain was the first U.S.-based coffee company to fully embrace a fair trade model. Today it is arguably one of the most vigilant corporate supporters of the crusade. Although competitors like Starbucks and Dunkin' Donuts have recently initiated fair trade programs of their own, Green Mountain has spent the past fourteen years nurturing a business model that sustains coffee farmer communities, while producing the highest-quality brew for coffee drinkers and healthy returns for shareholders.

The company continues to drive the growth of its $116 million coffee business by selling more than 8.4 million pounds of fair trade and farm-direct coffee each year. Though all the company's coffees are "ethically sourced," Green Mountain's farm-direct and fair trade lines represent ample economic benefits for coffee growers.[5] In 2002 these coffees represented more than 54 percent of the company's annual volume, making Green Mountain one of the largest fair trade coffee retailers in the United States.[6]

Since it adopted a fair trade model in the early 1990s, Green Mountain has become a poster child for the cause. Last year the company's fair trade efforts were profiled on PBS's *Frontline World* program, creating national recognition both for the company and for its socially responsible drive. The company also launched its own U.S.-based communications campaign by which it seeks to educate the public about the importance of ethically sourced products.

Green Mountain's fair trade efforts have earned it a range of industry tributes. In 2003 the company was rated number eight on *Business Ethics* magazine's 100 Best Corporate Citizens list. In 2001 *Forbes* named Stiller Entrepreneur of the Year, while in 2002 Green Mountain was placed on that publication's list of 200 Best Small Companies in America for the third year running.

In addition to being a leader in ethical standards across industries, the company is also on a fast track for growth. In 2003 Green Mountain's net sales were up 16.7 percent over 2002, indicating that healthy financial performance need not come at the expense of others. Stiller is quite convinced that

the opposite is true: "Our entrepreneurial spirit and commitment to corporate social responsibility, I believe, is the foundation for who we are and why we succeed."7 By disclosing the
nature of its responsible business programs, Green Mountain
is out to show the world how well an equitable model of commerce can work.

TRADING FAIRLY

Every business depends on healthy relationships to thrive.
Strong relationships with shareholders, employees, customers,
vendors, and suppliers naturally enable a company to compete
more efficiently. Therefore, it could be said that every business,
no matter what category it is in, is relationship driven.

Green Mountain Coffee shines in its approach to relationships. The company has demonstrated the value of treating all
people with respect, dignity, and compassion. All parties — no
matter what role they play for the company — are treated as
individuals instead of being clumped together as faceless
"employees," "customers" or "suppliers." At a fundamental
level, this is what trading fairly means. According to Stiller, to
trade fairly means to reject corporate indifference, to embrace
justice, and to harness the value of connection.

Green Mountain was the first coffee company to sign a
Memorandum of Understanding with the U.S. Agency for
International Development, under which it created an alliance
aimed at helping to mitigate the negative effects of the coffee
crisis. The company has also taken steps to counteract the pre-
cipitous decline in coffee prices by paying more for coffee than
it potentially could in the open market. Through its Steward-

ship program, the company pays coffee farmers a price that exceeds the cost of production and supports a reasonable livelihood. For fair trade–certified coffee, Green Mountain pays a floor price of $1.26 per pound, and for doubly certified fair trade organic coffee, it pays a floor price of $1.42 per pound — compared to the current commodity-based prices of 24 to 50 cents per pound.

However, as Stiller explains, a good price is only half the company's emphasis: "We believe in the power of community, that is, in our employees knowing personally the farmers who grow our coffee and the farmers knowing personally the people who roast and market their crops. This creates more motivational dynamics and a sense that we are really in this together. We're all connected through coffee."

Since 1992 Green Mountain has sent about 20 percent of its employees and a significant number of its customers on trips to coffee farms throughout Mexico and Central America. Stiller says that the company has done this to foster personal connections with farmer communities and to inspire pronounced dedication to the company's fair trade efforts. The approach worked, as Stiller explains: "It's one thing to understand the issues surrounding coffee farming on an intellectual level. But it's quite another to experience the circumstances first-hand. After someone comes back from a trip, we inevitably hear comments like 'I never fully understood this before' or 'I can't stand to see even one coffee bean wasted' or 'It changed my life.' People walk away with a whole new level of motivation."

> I've often observed that when we see people in need, it is human nature to want to come together and respond.
>
> — Bob Stiller

Dedication to the cause and loyalty to the company have also been the results of the trips taken by some of Green Mountain's largest grocery store chain customers. "Perry Odak, CEO of Wild Oats Market, recently traveled with me to Mexico, and I can tell you that he is now more than ever an advocate of fair trade–certified coffee," recalls Stiller.

In addition, farmers from coffee cooperatives are given opportunities to visit Green Mountain Coffee headquarters in Waterbury, Vermont. In a recent visit from a Sumatran coffee cooperative, employees heard some moving firsthand accounts from cooperative members: "They shared that their cooperative is a pocket of peace in Indonesia. Religious and cultural factions that have typically been archenemies have come together in peace to join the cooperative and support each other's efforts to make a living with coffee," says Stiller. "Several times their stories moved employees to tears."

PROVIDING SUSTENANCE

Green Mountain's management team knows many of the farmers who supply their beans by face, by name, and by story. They have listened to farmers' concerns and have responded in kind. But even more important, the company has enabled coffee community members to attain a better standard of living. Green Mountain has turned the coffee crisis into an opportunity by giving coffee growers a chance to bootstrap their way out of poverty. "Our goal is to develop programs that help coffee communities become more independent and less reliant on foreign aid. In many cases, this has meant assisting them in producing higher-quality coffee, which in turn enables them to command a higher price," says Stiller.

Within multiple coffee communities around the world, for instance, Green Mountain has developed cupping labs, which enable local farmers in coffee regions to taste-test their coffee before it ships. Cupping labs are a remarkable innovation, since relatively few coffee farmers actually taste their coffee brewed either in an American or European style.

> We work with communities to understand their most pressing needs and then support programs that have long-term, self-sustaining benefits.
>
> — Bob Stiller

Since one or two bad beans can ruin an entire batch, this quality-control method has become truly essential to the company and to coffee growers alike.

Green Mountain has also funded new drying patios in Guatemala as well as processing mills and hydroelectric power plants in Peru, enabling local coffee community members to produce a better product. In addition, the company extends zero- or low-interest preharvest loans to coffee growers, allowing them to make use of top-rate fertilizers and techniques. Stiller summarizes the rationale behind the company's coffee partner programs: "Our strategy has always been to ensure a long-term supply of high-quality coffee now and far into the future. Fortunately, we have been building relationships with a number of coffee estates and cooperatives that are able to produce the quality coffee we seek, despite market conditions."[8]

Green Mountain's helping hand extends to other areas besides coffee quality. The company donates 5 percent of its pretax profits to charities that serve coffee-growing communities and partners with outside organizations like Coffee Kids and Heifer International to provide these individuals with alternative income sources, such as livestock. "This helps lessen the impact of the coffee crisis and provides farmers with an ability to weather market forces, while also providing an additional source of food," says Stiller.

Just as Green Mountain's approach to fair trade includes more than a good price paid, it also extends beyond industry definitions. Fairtrade Labelling Organizations International (FLO) requires that all sources of coffee be democratically organized cooperative groups. This means that coffee monies are paid directly to these cooperative groups, then channeled to individual farmers as cooperative decision makers see fit. Smaller family-owned farms and independent growers who are not members of a cooperative are not eligible to sell fair trade–certified coffee. In response to these constraints, Green Mountain has developed a line of "farm-direct" coffees, enabling unqualified farmers to benefit directly from a fair approach to trade.

"Our farm-direct line of coffees represents a particularly high degree of intimacy and transparency between the company and our growers. We have developed multiyear supply and pricing agreements that are mutually beneficial, and we enable these farmers to benefit from our social and environmental project funding as well," notes Stiller. Currently, about 42 percent of Green Mountain's coffee is purchased farm direct, and given the success of the program, the company expects this proportion to increase well into the future.

On the whole, Stiller and his team have produced a system of trade that exceeds traditional industry standards on every possible level. In stark contrast to the trade systems used by much of the coffee industry (and other industries, for that matter), Green Mountain's approach benefits every participant in the supply chain. "All our partners — including farmers, producers, wholesale customers, and retailers — become more profitable, while consumers get high-quality coffee at a reasonable price, plus the chance to make a real contribution."

THE BENEFITS OF TRADING FAIRLY	
FOR COFFEE GROWER COMMUNITIES	A fair price gives coffee communities access to necessary nutrition, housing, health care, and education and enables farmers to reinvest in quality harvesting techniques. This, combined with the business skills developed as a result of working directly with coffee companies, helps to perpetuate a positive economic cycle.
FOR THE ENVIRONMENT	Since fair trade and farm-direct coffees are typically harvested in the shade using traditional and organic farming techniques, pesticides are rarely used, delicate ecosystems remain protected, and precious wildlife habitats, particularly for migratory birds, stay intact.
FOR COFFEE COMPANIES	In addition to tapping into rising media and consumer interest in ethically sourced products, fair trade or farm-direct programs enable coffee companies to develop stable, long-term relationships with coffee growers. This means that quality and consistency can be managed more efficiently, leading to a better product.
FOR COFFEE CONSUMERS	Fair trade and farm-direct coffees appeal to consumers who demand the best flavor. For a reasonable price, consumers can enjoy a better-quality coffee, and they know that their purchase has a positive impact on people around the world.

WHAT WOULD HAPPEN IF THE MAJORITY OF THE
U.S. COFFEE INDUSTRY SWITCHED TO A FAIR TRADE MODEL?

Stiller: Let's start with the coffee growers. If all coffee were purchased under fair trade terms, those six hundred thousand farmers in Latin America who have left their farms over the past year would return. This same pattern would take place in other parts of the world as well. While fair trade does not guarantee small-scale coffee farmers' prosperity, it does more than cover their costs. It provides them with the opportunity to meet the basic needs of their families and communities.

With fair trade pricing, cooperatives can choose to build a school that families can afford to send their children to. They can choose to build a medical clinic that families can afford to use. Fair trade does and will, in this scenario, enable farmers to reinvest in the quality of their coffee — allowing them to purchase needed materials, like fertilizer, that have a direct impact on coffee quality. Fair trade will eliminate hunger and fear of hunger in many coffee-growing areas and will bring stability to communities and to countries. The importance of these benefits cannot be overstated.

A shift to fair trade coffee would also help to alleviate the tremendous challenges faced by many fair trade cooperatives today. Last year coffee cooperatives on the fair trade registry produced 175 million pounds of coffee. Yet they were only able to sell 35 million pounds of coffee under fair trade terms, leaving the rest to be sold at whatever the market would pay. In addition, many cooperatives would like to be included on the fair trade registry but under current conditions cannot. Fairtrade Labelling Organizations International does not want to add any cooperatives unless the cooperative has a market for its coffee, since most cooperatives on the registry are only selling between 20 and 30 percent of their production under fair trade terms.

If fair trade were the rule, the industry would become

more sophisticated. Cupping labs, which ensure quality, would become commonplace, as would the participation and voice of coffee growers at industry forums held around the world. I expect that quality would be improved as farmers receive a sustainable return for their crops and are able to reinvest in quality.

Should fair trade become the standard for most coffee sold in the United States, then consumers will undergo perhaps the largest attitudinal shift. While they will benefit from the improved quality, and from knowing the impact of their fair trade coffee purchases, their understanding of this impact may generate a groundswell of interest in how other products they purchase are produced. They will begin to ask, "Where did this shirt come from?" "How much did it cost?" "How much was the woman who sewed it paid?" Consumers will demand more fair trade products. In addition to coffee the FLO has already started certifying tea, cocoa, bananas, citrus fruit, rice, honey, mangoes, brazil nuts, and even soccer balls.

MODEL RESULTS

Since 2000, the year that Green Mountain first began purchasing fair trade–certified coffee, the results of those purchases have steadily ascended. According to TransFair USA, Green Mountain has directly enabled at least sixty-four thousand farmers to improve their methods and to stay employed, while a total of at least three thousand people from around the world have benefited from the company's financial contributions and community-building programs.

Because of Green Mountain's fair trade purchases, more than $1 million has been channeled back to farmers and their families, and the company estimates that such monies were used to support:

- organic farm conversions
- coffee quality-control programs
- the construction of schools, roads, and health clinics
- alternative sources of income and nutrition
- improved housing and transportation
- portable water systems

In 2000 the company's fair trade purchases accounted for roughly 5 percent of the company's total coffee sales. Between 2001 and 2003, Green Mountain's fair trade sales grew to more than 11.8 percent. In 2004 Stiller estimates that fair trade sales will account for more than 15 percent of sales, while farm-direct coffees will represent another 50 percent of the company's total coffee purchases.

In reality, the socioeconomic results of Green Mountain's fair trade purchases should be multiplied several times over to account for the full impact of the company's efforts. Stiller indicates that Green Mountain is in the process of tracking the socioeconomic results of all its coffee purchases, not just those that qualify as fair trade. "Ultimately, our goal is to have a business model that is 100 percent sustainable," he says.

To date Green Mountain's model has led to measurable rewards for the company and its shareholders. As Stiller indicates, brand affinity is steadily mounting: "Our commitment to trading responsibly has really built loyalty. We receive messages regularly indicating how inspiring our values have been." Recent market feedback indicates a positive correlation between customers' understanding of the company's stance on the coffee crisis problem and a strong and lasting bond.

It seems that the more people understand what the company is doing and why, the more committed they become both to the company and to the fair trade cause and the more they spread the word to others, and so forth. "Each day more consumers are understanding the impact of their fair trade purchases, and many are sharing this information with their friends and neighbors," Stiller notes.

SELECT CONSUMER FEEDBACK FROM 2003

"I recently saw a PBS show concerning the plight of coffee growers in Guatemala. After learning about your company's efforts, I wanted to let you know that from now on, I will be purchasing Green Mountain Coffee exclusively."

"It is so great to see such an important product being made available to the public by such a large company. There are more concerned citizens out here than corporate America may know, and we will make purchases that benefit the planet when given the chance."

"It is such a pleasure to know that what I am drinking and enjoying is not at the cost of someone else and that there are people out there in the business world who care about others while making money."

SELECT EMPLOYEE FEEDBACK FROM 2003

"Hearing about people dying because coffee prices are so low is heart-wrenching. What we're doing with fair trade is outstanding. It's really making a difference in the world, and that's important to me. It's great to be involved with this company."

"With our commitment to social responsibility, and in particular, fair trade coffee, it's very easy for me to feel dedicated and excited about what I sell and represent. More important, it's easier to pass on that energy to prospective customers."

"In today's business world, it is indeed rare that just by coming to work you can feel truly in your heart that you are making a difference in the lives of those around you and making the world at large a better place."

Mounting brand loyalty certainly seems to have accelerated the company's financial performance. Today Green Mountain is one of the fastest-growing gourmet coffee brands in the country. In the fourth quarter of fiscal 2003, the company's net sales rose by 27.1 percent to $27,505,000, up from $21,641,000 in the fourth quarter of 2002, and the company expects to sustain a double-digit growth rate well into the future. In 2004 the goal is to achieve an annual growth rate of between 13 and 18 percent.

For more than a decade, the company has consistently reported positive results. "Twenty-two years ago, we began as one small café in Vermont. Today we are a $116-plus-million coffee roaster, with a multichannel business that is growing from a strong Northeast presence to the rest of the Eastern Seaboard and several other markets across the country. In fact, the majority of growth in fiscal 2003 came from outside the New England area as our brand, values, and the quality of our coffee gain increasing acceptance," comments Stiller.[9]

> It is our sincere hope that the success of our business model will compel the entire industry to adopt a new, more sustainable approach.
>
> — Bob Stiller

Green Mountain is clearly intent on converting big business to fair business: "There are some who argue that fair trade is not the answer to alleviating the social and economic problems created by the coffee industry, and I agree that it is not the only solution. But it is a great step forward and a policy that should be embraced by more coffee companies, particularly those with a large impact," proclaims Stiller.

DEFYING CONVENTION

Anita Roddick, founder of the London-based bath and beauty product giant The Body Shop, follows a similar calling. Like

Stiller, she seeks to make over the unflattering side of capitalism and to build an impermeable, worldwide business conscience. Though her approach to doing so is conspicuously unique. Whereas Stiller and others rely on evolution, Roddick calls for full-blown revolution: "We are constantly told that alternatives to the present capitalist system are not feasible. So what we need is a good old-fashioned dose of heresy. We need modern, corporate heretics," she proclaims.

Roddick is a risk taker. When given the choice between doing the right thing and facing the fire, or doing the wrong thing and staying safe, she always chooses the former: "If you're a corporate leader not fighting for human rights or trade justice, then what the *hell* are you doing? How do you feel that you have any rightful place in the business world? I just don't get apathy. I just don't get indifference."

Roddick has never been one to shy away from controversy. On the contrary, she has used it to get her messages across. Over the years, she has risked her reputation, her career, her company, her relationships, and even her life for her beliefs, and she routinely takes extreme steps to empathize more with those most negatively affected by the powers that be.

For example, Roddick lived on the streets of London for weeks, posing as a homeless person so that she could experience destitution firsthand. She has immersed herself in a range of cultures from the developing world, for months at a time, so that she could better identify the political and social ramifications of corporate strongholds. She fought side by side with controversial activists like the late Ken Saro-Wiwa, who — despite The Body Shop's efforts to save him — was reportedly murdered by the Nigerian military regime for exposing the surreptitious relationship between the regime and Royal Dutch Shell.[10]

Today Roddick continues to fight vigilantly for what she believes and has gained many fans and some powerful supporters as a result of her actions. Yet there are also those who believe that she goes too far (or not far enough, as the case may be), others who wish that she would keep her mouth shut, and still others who have gone to extremes to help her do just that. "I got into some dangerous territory when I started challenging some of the bigger corporations for what they were doing in developing countries. I remember [certain companies] hiring agents to intimidate me. They would harass me, play dirty tricks, go through my documents, sift through my trash cans, everything," claims Roddick.

> I guess since I'm a loudmouth, I wanted a loudmouth company that served to speak out for the voiceless.
>
> — Anita Roddick

Despite even the most outrageous attempts to stop her, Roddick presses on with her battle to end corporate injustices — leaving some industry insiders wondering whether she is indeed a certifiable lunatic or the only sane one left in the debate. "The way I see it, business is sort of the soul of international violence. I feel it is the cause of many wars now. Some of the biggest human rights abuses are conducted in the name of profits or in the name of particular corporations," says Roddick. "I am not opposed to trade, or to companies with foreign operations in lesser-developed nations. On the contrary. I'm simply concerned about quality in trade." The Body Shop, as she explains, was set up as an antidote to irresponsible trading practices.

The Body Shop's Community Trade Program engages more than thirty-five suppliers in twenty-five countries and specifically targets supplier communities that are disadvantaged in

some way. The company works directly with these communities to develop environmentally and financially sustainable
models for farming ingredients indigenous to a particular geographic region. These ingredients, ranging from marula oil
from Namibia to bananas from the Caribbean, are used to
make The Body Shop's bath and beauty products more exotic
and desirable. The efficient sourcing of these ingredients also
provides long-term socioeconomic benefits, as suppliers now
have the ability to provide their resources to global consumers,
and to other global retailers. "To our knowledge, The Body
Shop is the only commercial retailer which has a targeted purchasing program [such as this]," the company says. "[We] are
in a powerful position. By our words and actions, we can help
develop this focus on fair trade, increase awareness, and moti-
vate consumers to take action and to make a difference to disadvantaged communities by how they spend their money."[11]

Indeed, The Body Shop has created swift momentum for
the fair trade cause, not simply through its own trade programs but through novel communications campaigns that
pressure other companies to follow a similar path. Sure, they
sell environmentally friendly soap, moisturizer, and bubble
bath — but the real value of the company lies in its unique
ability to persuade people both to shop and to take political
action. Over the years, The Body Shop has encouraged its consumers to boycott certain companies, to protest, to sign peti-
tions, to lobby governments, and to use other activist tactics.
In doing so, they have created a captive audience and a distinctive, high-impact brand.

Today, despite a dizzying series of upheavals and financial
ups and downs, The Body Shop has realized Roddick's original
vision. The company is arguably one of the world's most spirited

For me, The Body Shop has always been less about product and more about communication. Conveying issues of importance like trade justice, human rights, political rights, and economic rights is what we do best.

— Anita Roddick

corporate supporters of trade justice and human rights, while Roddick herself is one of the most contentious. Although today she is less involved in the day-to-day operations of The Body Shop — having moved on to become a full-time environmental and social campaigner — a culture of commitment to solving vast social problems still thrives within the £697 million company, as it routinely uses its creative skills, resources, and 1,968 retail stores in fifty countries to get the word out to would-be consumer activists from around the globe.

MARKETING RIGHTEOUSLY

If the effectiveness of communication can be determined by how much it stirs people, then The Body Shop's approach to the fair trade cause may be considered a stunning success. Over the years, the inherent passion brewing in the company has given rise to some highly innovative and courageous approaches — leading to the participation of millions of consumers.

The company's campaigns are designed not to promote products or to tout a socially responsible track record but to directly engage consumers in the crusade to better the business world. The company tells people: "Businesses in particular have a part to play in effecting social change. If more businesses demonstrated a social conscience and acted with social responsibility, governments would have to listen. It's the big businesses who have the power over governments — and it's you, the individual consumer, who has the power over big business."[12]

Early on, The Body Shop realized that one of the most effective ways to get consumers personally involved was to outrage them, so several of the company's campaigns have called attention to the awful truths about business. "We wanted consumers to be clear about what we were up against. So we painted a picture of the existing climate," says Roddick. In this climate, as the company portrays it, multinationals routinely enter countries where environmental laws are loose, labor is cheap, and communities are desperate. Then they leave nothing behind but toxic waste and embittered workers.[13]

One of the best examples of The Body Shop's salient communication style was its 1998 Make Your Mark campaign. Make Your Mark, which celebrated the fortieth anniversary of the Universal Declaration of Human Rights, ran in conjunction with Amnesty International. It was aimed at raising public awareness of the human rights abuses associated with big business. To do this, the company called the public's attention to the bravest of all human rights defenders: those who have risked everything to stand up to corporations and political cartels.

> To be serious about corporate ethics is to step out of line with the prevailing vision that now dominates the globe.
>
> — Anita Roddick

These defenders included Zafaryab Ahmed, a Pakastani journalist arrested for opposing child labor; Dita Indah Sari, an Indonesian woman arrested for calling for a minimum wage; Asma Jahangir, a Pakistani woman harassed for defending women's rights; and the "Ogoni 19," a group of activists detained for protesting corporate abuses and government corruption in Nigeria. Since many of the depicted human rights defenders were imprisoned and facing torture or death sentences, this campaign created a strong and lasting impression.

Because of its controversial and complex nature, Make Your

Mark had to be painstakingly planned and executed. After anchoring the campaign's core messages and defining desired results, the company conducted a series of brainstorming sessions with members of Amnesty International. These sessions were designed to generate breakthrough creative ideas from as many viewpoints as possible, while ensuring buy-in across both organizations. Next, since much of the campaign was to be implemented in The Body Shop's stores, the company consulted with almost every senior executive from across The Body Shop organization to flag potential obstacles and to refine the creative work around particular market needs.

THE BODY SHOP'S HUMAN RIGHTS CAMPAIGN TIME LINE

1988: Established key relationships with suppliers in developing countries, leading to a company-wide policy of fair trade. (The program was initially named Trade Not Aid. It is now called Community Trade.)

1988: Launched its first international human rights campaign with Amnesty International.

1989: Ran a campaign with Survival International dedicated to depicting the plight of Brazil's indigenous Yanomami, who were threatened by the destruction of their lands by mining and timber companies.

1991: Founded the *Big Issue*, a newspaper that worked to enable thousands of homeless people to realize their right to housing through Trade Not Aid.

1993: Campaigned vigorously in support of Ken Saro-Wiwa and the Ogoni people of Nigeria, who were protesting the economic and environmental destruction caused by the Nigerian military dictatorship and multinational oil companies such as Shell.

1995: Following the execution of Ken Saro-Wiwa, redoubled its efforts to educate the public and bring about political change in Nigeria. These efforts climaxed when Ken's son attended the Commonwealth Heads of Government meeting in New Zealand, inspiring global world leaders to take action.

1996: Shifted the Ogoni campaign to focus on defending the lives of the Ogoni 19, a group of political prisoners facing the same charges as Ken Saro-Wiwa. The public relations and advertising campaign ran in seventeen countries and won Best International Campaign of the Year at the U.K. PR Week Awards ceremony. In September that year, these prisoners were set free, and charges against them were dropped, partly as a result of The Body Shop's efforts.

1998: Celebrated the fiftieth anniversary of the Universal Declaration of Human Rights by joining forces with Amnesty International to launch Make Your Mark, the world's largest human rights campaign. More than three million Body Shop customers in more than thirty countries participated by signing a petition in support of the human rights cause.

2000: Launched The Body Shop Human Rights Awards biannual program as a way to call international attention to the individuals and organizations responsible for making the most significant strides in the realm of human rights. The key issue highlighted was the estimated 250 million youngsters trapped in child labor situations.

2002: Held the second Body Shop Human Rights Awards ceremony to acknowledge the most significant strides made in the fight for the right to housing. The ceremony rewarded those individuals and groups that best tackled issues like forced displacement, discrimination, and the rights of indigenous peoples with a $300,000 cash prize.

Taken from www.thebodyshop.com.

The Body Shop also gave employees the ability to project their views by enabling each retail store manager to select his or her own human rights defender. Across thirty-four separate markets, thousands of store managers effectively launched their own minicrusades for the human rights hero of their choice. The stores engaged consumers through print materials and merchandising, and organized in-store events — giving visitors the chance to ask questions and interact with Body Shop and Amnesty representatives directly. And to draw consumers in even closer to the cause, The Body Shop created an innovative petition on which consumers left their thumbprint (rather than simply a signature) as a symbolic way to lend support. These consumer thumbprints later served as the primary visual element of the print advertising campaign, as the company turned them into giant portraits of the human rights defenders as depicted by local artists from participating markets.

> It wasn't rocket science. We just knew how to market the human rights issues better than most nonprofits. We had the best practices and the creative abilities already in place, and we just put them to work for the cause.
>
> — Anita Roddick

"The key to the success of this campaign was that everyone within the organization felt a part of it. We turned each of our shops into action stations. We really educated our employees," Roddick recalls. "I remember going into The Body Shop store in Picadilly Square in the center of London shortly after several prisoners that we had campaigned for were released from prison. The manager of the store, who had fought for a Moroccan prisoner of conscience, came up to me and put her hands on my shoulders. She said, 'This is the real me.' I knew that she wasn't talking about moisture cream. She sensed that she had helped to change the world. And indeed, she had."

Following the local in-store events, Make Your Mark was launched as a global campaign. With the participation of His Holiness the Dalai Lama of Tibet, The Body Shop held a major launch event in Atlanta, Georgia, garnering tremendous media coverage. The launch was covered internationally by forty-three television stations in fifteen countries. And as a follow-up to the launch, the company organized a finale in a Paris art gallery to highlight the unveiling of the finished defender portraits.

Because the campaign enabled the release of several human rights defenders, three were able to attend the event, providing a powerful symbolic end to the campaign. Then, as an encore, the company sponsored Amnesty International's anniversary concert, which featured performances by Bruce Springsteen, Peter Gabriel, Radiohead, Alanis Morissette, and Tracy Chapman. The Body Shop was acknowledged by the fifteen thousand concert attendees — along with millions of others who heard the broadcast.

Given the precision, scale, and significance of the Make Your Mark campaign, both the company and the cause benefited greatly. "The level of consumer participation was truly remarkable," says Roddick. Overall, the company estimates that the campaign's media coverage reached more than 1 billion people worldwide. The Body Shop ended up collecting more than three million consumer thumbprints — amounting to about 2,700 per participating store. In addition, two hundred thousand consumers sent protest cards to corporate and government groups seemingly connected with human rights violations, and another 2,100 joined Amnesty International. And, most impressive, eight of the twelve human rights defenders highlighted through the Make Your Mark campaign publicly stated that the campaign had helped them directly. One of these defenders reportedly escaped death, while several others were released from prison.

RODDICK'S GUIDE TO INSPIRING CONSUMER AND EMPLOYEE ACTIVISM

- Be vigilant and brave. Don't be afraid to bend the rules. There are risks involved in taking a stand, but unless more companies do, we have little hope of evolving.
- Communicate with passion. You've got to bring out people's inner fire. Consumers and employees are just waiting to feel engaged, so give them a good reason.
- Educate people. Don't just talk about what should be done; show people how values, or the lack thereof, work in reality. The truth is the most potent medicine.
- Engage the support of nonprofit organizations. They know more about the cause than you, and they can serve as your most valuable advisers and strategic partners.
- Leverage company assets. Whatever your company's greatest strength, be it creativity, infrastructure, or technology, use it to drive your crusade.

Despite the success of this and other Body Shop campaigns, onlookers still ask, "What in the world do human rights have to do with beauty products?" In answer to these uncertainties, Roddick vigorously asserts: "Despite the enormous need for it, no company has ever stood for human rights. No company has ever challenged other powerful multinationals on the basis of their human rights violations. We did. And we will continue to do so. Because if we don't, who will?"

The company's more recent human rights–related communications have ventured into territory that hits a bit closer to

home: domestic violence. The international campaign Stop
Violence in the Home currently runs in the United States,
Europe, Asia, and Canada and positions
domestic violence as a critical self-
esteem and human rights issue. In typical Body Shop fashion, the campaign
urges people to "break the silence" and
to do something about the problem by
"help(ing) our friends or loved ones in
need." The company encourages women
and asserts that "every family deserves
the right to live and love without fear."[14]

> The Body Shop stands for
> more than a moisturizer and
> profits. It stands for moral
> leadership. We will continue
> to fight for positive change
> because we know that what
> we do affects millions.
>
> — Anita Roddick

In addition to hard-line campaigns and a Community
Trade initiative, The Body Shop's human rights program also
includes a biennial award ceremony committed to highlighting
the accomplishments of global pioneers in the human rights
field. Steve McIvor, the company's Head of Values, explains the
wider purpose of the company's efforts: "Our human rights
program is a powerful and practical expression of our ongoing
commitment to enabling social change. It has made a real contribution to the movement over the years, and in doing so, it
has enhanced our company culture and our brand."

However, devoting a very public business to the pursuit of
radical change has its downside. It's not a course for the faint
of heart. "To force change in the business world, you've got to
be a thought leader. You've got to be a forerunner. You've got
to go where others refuse to. And you've got to prove it can be
done," says Roddick. "One thing I've learned the hard way is that
you've got to put all your money where your mouth is. The
minute you dedicate yourself to an aspiration, the press will be
waiting for you to slip up. The press loves the smell of hypocrisy,

because that's what sells. That's how writers get their fame. So they will crucify you for anything they perceive as a mistake."

FACING THE FIRE

Despite The Body Shop's accomplishments, it continues to receive flak from critics intent on proving a disparity between the company's do-gooder image and its daily practices. Since the mid-1990s, numerous reporters have accused The Body Shop of falsely indicating that all its ingredients are completely natural; of discharging factory pollutants into the New Jersey water system; of purchasing supplies from countries, such as China, that it had protested on the basis of human rights violations; of undermining its own Community Trade policy by channeling skimpy payments to suppliers in developing countries; and of making too few philanthropic donations.[15]

> Our biggest mistake was being too enthusiastic. In the beginning, we wanted to do everything on our own. We were in such a hurry to make change, that in some cases our ambition got ahead of what we could feasibly do.
>
> — Anita Roddick

Though Roddick questions the true motivations of these reporters, the company admits that some of their accusations are true. "Two minor spillages in New Jersey occurred in January and June of 1992. The spillages involved thirty gallons of Orange Spice Shampoo and thirty gallons of Fuzzy Peach Shower Gel. In both cases, we reported the spills as required," says McIvor. Similarly, regarding the China incident, Roddick concedes: "I spoke out against China at a time when we did source certain supplies from them. And so certain people called us hypocrites. But we were clear in that we did commit Chinese suppliers to our Code of Conduct.

We have always put human rights and social justice at the very beginning of our trade relationships." McIvor interjects: "Rather than boycott countries that have poor human rights records like China, we work to achieve positive change. Our Code of Conduct is based on international labor conventions that outline the standards we expect our suppliers to adhere to."

With respect to the natural ingredients claim, McIvor grants: "The Body Shop does not claim that our products are 100 percent natural. We would not be able to manufacture all-natural products with consistently high quality and a long shelf life without the use of some synthetics. We constantly look for ways to avoid the use of synthetic chemicals where feasible. Whenever we find a viable alternative, we reformulate."

Roddick protests that criticisms against the company's Community Trade program were also blown out of proportion. "When I first developed relationships with small, developing communities that eventually led to our Community Trade program, I didn't make my intentions absolute enough. Intentions on both sides were misinterpreted, I think. In retrospect, I should have more clearly expressed what I was and what I wasn't looking for," Roddick reflects. "But remember, we created the first fair trade program in our industry. We were literally carving new territory. So some trial and error was inevitable." McIvor agrees: "It hasn't been easy, but Community Trade remains a cornerstone of our business. Between 2002 and 2003, we spent nearly £5 million on this program. More than five hundred of our products now contain an ingredient sourced from communities in need. The program has helped to support thousands of people across the globe by building livelihoods for their families."

The company's philanthropic milestones seem to counter critics' accusations. Between 1990 and today, the company has donated more than £8 million to progressive and influential charity groups like Children on the Edge, the Ogoni, Born Free Foundation, and the Amazon Co-op. Combined with the fact that the company channels its profits back into expensive international campaigns that press for human rights, the cessation of domestic violence and animal testing, and increased environmental responsibility, this indicates an honorable intent. Besides, how many other companies have ever been so bold? How many other companies have taken such risks to inspire consumers and to move the rest of the business world in a more positive direction? The answer is, remarkably few. The Body Shop is certainly not faultless. But it is also one of the corporate world's bravest.

EXTRAORDINARY RESULTS

Since its founding in 1988, The Body Shop has built a strong, internationally recognized brand while helping to save lives and ways of life. The company's communications campaigns have worked to create significant change: "I certainly know that we saved twenty Ogoni lives in Nigeria. I certainly know that we've sustained entire communities with fair trade relationships. I certainly know that we have had a great deal of fun going in the opposite direction of the beauty business," says Roddick.[16]

Through its campaigning and fair trade–related efforts, the company estimates that it has made a real and measurable difference to the human rights cause. Specifically, The Body Shop has

- helped save the lives of multiple political prisoners facing death sentences and helped free others from prison;

- reached well over a billion consumers with inspirational messages regarding the importance of issues like child labor, economic exploitation, trade justice, indigenous rights, gender equality, and the right to housing;

- generated global publicity and channeled $900,000 to grassroots human rights organizations through ongoing awards events;[17]

- enabled thousands of families in developing countries to gain access to better nutrition, health care, and housing through ongoing Community Trade programs;

- publicly challenged major corporations including Nike, Shell Oil, and ExxonMobil for alleged human rights and environmental-related misdeeds in foreign countries.

Over the years, The Body Shop's social initiatives have matured from fly-by-night protests to increasingly sophisticated, brand-building programs. As a result, consumers have grown more engaged. A recent Omnibus study conducted for the company indicated that of those who were aware of The Body Shop, the vast majority agreed that the company cared deeply for the environment and for its consumers, while 21 percent of respondents indicated that their main reason for purchasing Body Shop products was the company's strong ethical stance.

After a period of negative press and financial difficulty,

which lasted from 1999 through 2002, The Body Shop has enjoyed an improved performance record. In 2003 the company reported solid progress across multiple areas. Compared to 2002, company sales were up 2 percent, earnings per share were up 143 percent, and net debt was reduced by £21 million. "This year, we have worked on shaping and strengthening our organizational structure and have created a strong culture of accountability and responsibility, allowing us to focus on delivering value to our customers and all our stakeholders," remark Executive Chairman Adrian Bellamy and CEO Peter Saunders in their 2003 letter to shareholders: "The Body Shop culture of campaigning for social and environmental change is core to the business."[18]

In founding this business, we wanted to use a new language of measurement — where our success would be deemed not by profit and loss, but by our wider contributions to society.

— Anita Roddick

For Roddick, stronger sales and improved operations are less a cause for celebration and more a route to enhanced social impact. "We always wanted our business to be more for public good than private greed. And overall, I think we have been. I'm proud of what we have been able to accomplish over the years." She offers a word of advice to socially minded entrepreneurs thinking about starting their own businesses: "Remember that going public presents its challenges. The stock market doesn't allow you freedom or time for reflection. It doesn't allow you room to properly strategize. Because the bigger you get, the more you get forced into bigness when really you should be forced into brilliance or forced into bravery or forced into something else."

WHY DO CORPORATIONS CONTINUE TO
COMMIT HUMAN RIGHTS VIOLATIONS?

Roddick: The reason that companies still commit human rights violations is that they are allowed to. There is no law in the World Trade Organization (WTO) that says that a product with a human rights violation attached to it shall not be allowed into the marketplace. We have far more laws regarding the use of a logo or a brand name than we do protecting the lives of fifteen-year-old children making the particular product at hand. There's no law to protect indigenous rights. There's no law to protect the environment. Nothing. It's all about the ease with which companies can trade.

If it were the other way around, then many big companies would have been penalized out of business long ago. But they're too busy maximizing profits and offering the poorer communities in America a cheaper and cheaper product. Many of the biggest companies in the world produce cheap goods on the backs of slaves.

Then you have the complicity of the press, which doesn't want to open up these cans of worms to the public, especially in America, because of the fact that the media is controlled by the very advertisers committing the violations in the first place. They're certainly not going to expose this stuff, so it's left to the alternative media. On top of that, you have governments, who are also in bed with corporations for obvious reasons. So the change is left up to the businesses themselves, who despite the urgent need for change continue to sink their standards to the lowest common denominator. They do anything that saves money or time.

The only possible hope for change is that enough consumers will stand together and demand it. Consumers are the conceivers of change because they can boycott, protest, campaign, and try to change the law. Their voice is the most powerful instrument, and they have intellectuals, religious organizations, and hundreds of NGOs and trade justice organizations on their side. There's a grassroots movement that's under way all around the world, and I believe that this is a very exciting moment.

Consumers are standing up against the largest companies in the world. More and more of them believe that the world should not be run by a handful of corporations. People are waking up, and they want to know under what conditions their products are made. For the first time ever, we have the biggest sense of collective outrage. Issues like child slavery are becoming high profile, and that is the key to change.

SPIRITUALITY IN BUSINESS?

Green Mountain Coffee Roasters and The Body Shop go against the grain in their goal to solve the most troubling problems caused by bad business practices. Green Mountain primarily uses business policies to inspire change from the top down, serving as a shining example to others who may follow. The Body Shop uses words to activate people, inspiring change from the grassroots level up. Both companies have made tremendous strides in their respective areas, and both have reinvigorated the social responsibility movement.

Though their personal expressions are worlds apart, Stiller and Roddick share an extraordinary belief. Both swear that spirituality can play a clear role in today's business world, if one defines spirituality not in religious or esoteric terms, but in human terms. Stiller explains: "For businesses to be successful in the long run, they need to take everyone into consideration. They have to realize that they are a piece of something much larger and more significant. All of us have to begin to think collectively, as a unified part of one planet." Roddick agrees: "We can pretend that our businesses operate independent of the world around us, or we can develop a greater sense of awareness and compassion for humanity and all living things."

Perhaps the question that the business community should be asking is not simply, "Why should we implement more responsible and compassionate business practices?" but rather, "Why *shouldn't* we?" Stiller and Roddick assert that business leaders make irresponsible decisions when they fail to acknowledge the impact that their actions have on wider stakeholder communities. And they make responsible decisions when they do the opposite. Would you rather get rich by helping or by harming your constituents? In your quest to be successful, would you rather focus on exclusive self-interest or the collective best interest? These leaders argue that for every business and every businessperson, both choices are there for the making.

As the Body Shop and Green Mountain stories indicate, the value of a company can be maximized when that company serves the best collective interests. Improving relationships with employees, suppliers, local communities, and the earth has obvious social value. In serving the needs of the whole, businesses can also create a competitive edge that translates to financial value. Today more than ever, companies need to make doubly sure that they are indeed adding instead of diminishing both forms of value through all their actions. This is what a focus on stakeholders really means.

WHAT IS THE ROLE OF SPIRITUALITY IN BUSINESS?	
BOB STILLER	ANITA RODDICK
"If you're going to equate spirituality with interconnectedness, then the role is clear. There is a commonality of interest that goes beyond the conventional boundaries of race, politics, or religion. Everyone on the planet has the basic need to survive. When we, as part of a company, appreciate the extent to which others need our help to survive, it opens a door to better solutions. Business is perhaps the most effective institution in the world. But until we as business leaders respond to the inequities that exist as a result of our current capitalist system, our own success and stability will remain hindered."	"One isn't one without the other. We've got to be kinder. We've got to be looking after the weak and the frail. Businesses should ask the questions, Is there anything we can do to make people's lives easier? Is there anything we can do to keep the communities we depend on intact? Is there anything we can do to keep cultures and the environment intact? Is there anything we can do to help develop a sustainable democracy? I think we need to start by asking more fundamental questions and offering ourselves room to experiment with creative answers. Because the truth is, business is just as much a social science as it is a financial science."

CHAPTER FIVE

NEED CYCLING

The Grameen Bank • Hewlett-Packard

True development puts those first that society puts last.

— **Mohandas Gandhi**

Historically, corporations have all but ignored the world's poor as a potential market opportunity. As the Grameen Bank and Hewlett-Packard demonstrate, however, improving the plight of this majority of the world's population represents an opportunity, not merely for philanthropy but also for business growth. These two companies show how elevating the socioeconomic status of the poor can build bridges between nations, improve the lives of millions, and drive sustainable profit. They uncover new routes for global firms willing both to increase their contact with and to enlarge their impact on the developing world.

Approximately 60 percent of the world's population, or upwards of 4 billion people, live in poverty.[1] These individuals spend their lives searching for food and shelter, fighting for physical survival, and fearing for the future. They exist with no access to health care or education, and with little or no political representation or freedom. More than 100 million impoverished children throughout the world remain uneducated, while another twenty-nine thousand under the age of five die every day from malnutrition and preventable diseases. Experts on global poverty warn us that, despite the hundreds of government groups, research institutions, and nonprofits dedicated to alleviating the situation, the poverty epidemic grows worse as the population of the developing world expands.

Given the web of economic, political, and social complexities enveloping the issue, many remain skeptical about the prospect of a poverty-free world. The problem, it seems, is too vast and beyond our control. But to one world-renowned economist in Bangladesh, Dr. Muhammad Yunus, this assumption is unjustified. Based on his experience working directly with the poorest of the poor, Yunus contends that the problem isn't nearly as insurmountable as we have been led to believe.

"Poverty isn't a space science, or about an intricate design of a complicated machine. It is a topic about people. I don't see the possibility of a human being becoming a 'problem' when it comes to his or her own well-being," he says. Yunus has spent the past thirty years perfecting a "microcredit" system that has worked to assist 3.12 million Bangladeshi citizens in creating a more productive future for themselves and their families. "I am totally convinced that poor people can get themselves out of poverty if we give them the same or similar opportunities that we give to others. The poor themselves can create a poverty-free world."[2]

Ever since Yunus was a professor of economics at Chittagong University in Bangladesh, he has taken poverty alleviation into his own hands. In 1974, shortly after Bangladesh had achieved independence from Pakistan, Yunus was baffled about why his country's newfound liberation didn't lead to the economic growth and diminished poverty levels that economists had predicted. "Instead of improving, things grew worse. People were dying in the streets, and there were hundreds of thousands without food, sick, and about to die," he recalls. "I had to find a new solution to the problem, because it was clear that what I was teaching in the classroom was not relevant. It was not helping in any way."

> What good is our current economic model if we cannot sustain the poor? Perhaps poverty is not the real problem; it's our mindset and systems that are fundamentally flawed.
>
> — Muhammad Yunus

Intent on discovering an answer, Yunus took his class into the real world, starting with visits to local Bangladeshi villages. One of the first people they encountered was a woman named Sufiya who made bamboo stools. Sufiya, the class discovered, had to borrow money to buy the raw bamboo required to make her stools from a middleman who charged her finance rates as high as 10 percent per week. At this rate, she was left with only a fractional profit margin. "Borrowers like Sufiya helped me to realize that the financial mechanisms available to the poor were only making them poorer," says Yunus. "I began to understand that these borrowers were desperate to increase their economic standing — if only to survive — and that if given the opportunity to borrow under humane terms and interest rates, they would do so. Moreover, I believed that these borrowers, particularly women, would repay their loans. They would struggle to be as faithful as possible to an institution that allowed them to borrow on fair terms."

After this visit and subsequent ones to villagers facing similar situations, Yunus reached into his own pocket and lent Sufiya and forty-two other local basket weavers a total of $27. "There I was, an economics professor, talking about millions or billions of dollars in the classroom, without realizing that what local people really needed was less than $1 apiece," he recalls. "So I lent this small amount of money and told the borrowers that they could pay me back whenever they could. To them, this was something of a miracle." Yunus was eventually paid back, while the borrowers themselves were able to amass enough of a financial cushion to lift themselves and their families above the poverty line.

Those tiny loans helped shape the Grameen Bank, an internationally recognized financial institution that operates in 43,681 impoverished villages throughout Bangladesh and the rest of the developing world. To date, Grameen has disbursed roughly $4.18 billion dollars to destitute borrowers, 94 percent of whom are women. Grameen is not a charity program. It charges borrowers interest rates of nearly 20 percent and imposes strict terms. Yet the bank boasts a 99.06 percent recovery rate on its loans, which is significantly higher than the rates experienced by most of the traditional banking world.

Since the Grameen Bank was officially founded in 1976, it has lifted hundreds of thousands out of poverty, grown the Bangladeshi economy, and achieved financial profitability. In 2003 Grameen's revenues reached $60.98 million, while offerings spanned to include low-interest personal loans, housing loans, microenterprise loans, scholarships, and educational loans. "It's a very powerful system, particularly in countries prone to poverty and natural disasters. It works to save people in trouble. Instead of relying on handouts, the people get back on their feet and become independent," Yunus contends. "We generate a very positive cycle of self-sufficiency."

Throughout his career, Yunus has remained vehement about the underlying causes of poverty. "One can reasonably state that people are poor today because of the failure of the financial institutions to support them in the past," he says. He also argues that foreign aid is less apt to accelerate economies or to improve people's lives, particularly in developing nations like Bangladesh. "If you look in our villages and among the poor families who live in them, you will find no imprint of [financial] assistance on their faces. For the most part, it was spent on foreign consultants, contractors, bureaucrats, and the purchase of equipment. The only people benefiting from this aid are those who are already wealthy, though they do so in the name of the poor," he says.3 What is needed, Yunus believes, is a direct investment in local people to create entrepreneurial opportunities and economic growth from the bottom up.

> Credit is a fundamental human right. Every person deserves something to work with to survive and become resourceful. If we don't allow people to seize their potential, society will never improve.
>
> — Muhammad Yunus

Yunus's antiestablishment sentiments, along with Grameen's unconventional banking model, have provoked a skeptical response in some quarters of the traditional business world. Western media have published numerous articles questioning the value and viability of microcredit. As recently as 2001, the *Wall Street Journal* published an article disparaging the Grameen Bank's accounting system, suggesting that the bank's repayment rate was in fact significantly lower than the organization claimed.4 Yunus denies this charge, asserting that the publication misconstrued data and misunderstood the bank's principles. "The press often supposes that we are hiding things, or that we are dysfunctional on some level. They tend to look at us with great suspicion and sometimes suggest that we are not a legitimate bank. The truth is that we are simply a different kind of bank. We have a different theory, different goals, and different terminologies," says Yunus. "It's like comparing European football with American football."

Over the years, Grameen has faced religious, political, and legal detractors as well. Empowering women, enabling the poor to rise to a new economic level, and decentralizing the source of power are concepts subversive enough to cause vigorous opposition in most countries, particularly one like Bangladesh. "Islamic leaders have accused us of damaging their religion, while political leaders have labeled us as antiestablishment and even dangerous revolutionaries. Initially, many people thought that we were conspirators, so they treated us like enemies," Yunus recalls. "They attacked us in any way that they could."

Yet, despite his critics, Yunus, who sources say is being considered for a Nobel Prize in economics, remains intent on demonstrating the value of his ideas to the developed world. "The fact is that mainstream society does not allow underprivileged people to explore their full potential," he says. Through microcredit, Yunus intends to reverse this trend. "My original hope for Grameen was that it would dispel poverty and hunger at their origin, and that by discussing the sources of poverty, we would develop better approaches for eliminating it. Today I believe that we have created not only a tool that ends poverty, but also one that does so in a sensible and profitable manner."

NEED CYCLING

Banking is a commercial industry like many others in the developed world. Though it serves a fundamental purpose, offerings are built around legalities and industry and company requirements rather than around people's needs. For instance, loans are typically issued to customers with the most collateral and the best financial histories, not to the poor or to the people who need credit most. Transactions tend to be complicated. Interest rates are often compounded. And payment schedules are rarely customized to fit individual situations. "The world has changed dramatically over the years, and society's problems have grown worse, but conventional banks still work the same way," remarks Yunus. "Maybe it's not that people are not credit worthy but that banks are not people worthy."

The Grameen Bank's most striking feature is its ability to meet unsatisfied socioeconomic needs in a lucrative way. To Yunus, the world's neediest are the ideal target market. "More than half the world's population is deprived of the services offered by conventional banks. There are literally billions of people in need of institutions that cater to their circumstances," he claims. "I believe that in terms of credit, the rules of banking should be reversed. The less you have, the higher your priority." Yunus also asserts that the most desperate customers pose the best financial risk, and that they are well poised to productively improve economic and social conditions for future generations: "Our borrowers cannot afford not to repay their loans. For many of them, this loan is the only chance they will have to end a cycle of poverty for their families. They must put it to good use. There is no margin of error."

In qualifying its customers, Grameen looks for human potential, an asset Yunus perceives to be far more significant than any financial capital or collateral. "We must recognize that every person has an inner strength, even if he or she can't display it because of current circumstances," he claims. "The poor can do so much with so little. Given the opportunity, they can become incredibly innovative and resourceful."

> We recognized that the poor were not only worth the risk, but that they were more accountable and resourceful than traditional borrowers. As a result, we have a better growth rate than any other bank in Bangladesh and than most in the United States.
>
> — Muhammad Yunus

Grameen is counting on the ingenuity of its borrowers to spread positive economic influence throughout communities and eventually, the rest of the world. "We see the poor as human bonsai trees," Yunus explains. "If a healthy seed of a giant tree is planted in a flowerpot, the tree that will grow will be a miniature version of the giant tree. There is no fault in the seed. The seed was simply denied a base to grow on. People are poor because society has denied them a real social and economic base to grow on. They are given only small flowerpots." Grameen's purpose, Yunus explains, is to move these seeds from the pot to the soil of society so that they can grow, thrive, and eventually become influential in and of themselves. "One day we hope to enjoy the shade these trees produce."

This bonsai analogy crystallizes Yunus's vision of trickle-up economics. By issuing the poor credit for self-employment, the Grameen Bank effectively creates jobs, promotes trade, and sustains local entrepreneurs. Collectively, these entrepreneurs begin to work together and assert their influence on local culture, economies, and government bodies until their impact is broad enough to influence laws, global business practices, and the political and economic status of nations. According to Yunus, this cycle is the key to solving the poverty problem once and for all: "These millions of small people with their millions of small pursuits can add up to create the biggest development wonder."[5]

HOW GRAMEEN INVERTS TRADITION	
CONVENTIONAL BANKING	**GRAMEEN BANKING**
Profit-driven enterprise	Social-market enterprise
Caters to men	Caters to women
Management owned	Customer owned
Product-centric	People-centric
Procedure orientation	Relationship orientation
Based on legal instruments	Based on trust
Requires collateral	Encourages potential
Pre-set terms	Customized terms

WORTHY OF IMITATION

The Grameen Bank is an anomaly, its methodology the antithesis of traditional banking principles. "Conventional banks are focused on rich men, whereas we are focused on poor women. Conventional banks look at what has already been achieved by a person, whereas we look at what is waiting to be unleashed. Conventional banks are focused on maximizing profits, whereas we are focused on helping people to become financially stable," Yunus recounts. However, despite these stark differences, Grameen's model presents valuable elements that are worth replicating within the wider financial-services industry and beyond.

For instance, Grameen is by nature a hybrid company. It is not a profit-driven enterprise that serves the exclusive financial interests of shareholders. Nor is it a social enterprise that reinvests the bulk of its revenues back into the community.

"We represent a third category, which I call a social-market enterprise," describes Yunus. "Our borrowers own 93 percent of the bank. This means that we serve our shareholders and society at the same time — without the conflicts of interest typically encountered by organizations trying to do both. If borrowers are happy, the bank makes a profit and the profit gets funneled back to the owners."

This factor has been a key to the Grameen's ability to oper-ate successfully. Not only has the bank amassed enough wealth to keep shareholders content, but individual shareholders have amassed enough wealth, potential, and ambition to accelerate the bank's growth. According to Yunus, most of Grameen's borrowers stay committed for life. "Once we help a woman explore and seize her immediate opportunities, she tends to concentrate on the second generation within her family. She begins to seek other avenues of financing for education or housing," he explains. "Today many of our customers have pen-sion funds and savings accounts, and almost all send their chil-dren to school using Grameen scholarships or educational assistance. In addition, our housing loans have been used to build more than half a million homes."

Funding for emergencies, education, and housing in turn breeds further stability and economic growth. By issuing credit, Grameen reverses the age-old vicious circle of low income, low savings, and low investment into a virtuous circle of low income, injection of credit, investment, more income, more savings, more investment, more income.[6] "When poor people have a dry floor and roof over their head, they tend to become particularly active, spend additional time at work, and ultimately earn more," asserts Yunus.

Grameen has developed a customer service approach that is

truly needs oriented. The bank's "flexi-loan" is customized to fit the borrower's situation and abilities, ensuring that the borrower can pay back the loan in a timely manner.7 "Instead of punishing struggling borrowers through legal intervention the way traditional banks do, we help people overcome their problems," says Yunus. "We work with borrowers to reschedule their loans without making them feel as if they have done something wrong, because indeed, they have not." According to Yunus, the technique works, since the majority of flexi-loan borrowers pay back their loans at an accelerated pace — often several times faster than repayment schedules require.

> Whereas conventional banks don't worry about what happens to their borrowers in terms of livelihood or social standing, we rely on positive socioeconomic change to prosper as a company.
>
> — Muhammad Yunus

Interest rates were also up for revision. Grameen has structured simple terms in accordance with the needs of its borrowers. "Interest on conventional bank loans is generally compounded quarterly and can often be a multiple of the principle, depending on the length of the loan period," says Yunus. "We knew that this was an impossible provision." Instead, Grameen guarantees that the total interest accrued on each loan it disburses never exceeds the amount of the loan, regardless of how long it takes borrowers to repay. Thus, rather than be dragged into further debt over time, Grameen borrowers rely on simpler transactions.

Another aspect of Grameen's needs orientation is its unusual approach to managing customer relationships through bank branches. In Bangladesh, a country where travel is difficult and villages are greatly spread out, Grameen decided that to do business effectively, borrowers should never have to leave their homes. The bank's "bicycle bankers," as they have now become known, instead make routine house calls. "We have twelve thousand staff routinely going out to forty-four thousand villages throughout Bangladesh to meet our borrowers at their doorsteps," Yunus says. "It's about being an institution that is in the presence of the people, rather than having the people in the presence of the institution."

Business wisdom might suggest that measures like these can undermine a company's operational viability. However, Grameen has developed some infallible mechanisms that keep customers reliable and revenues flowing predictably. For example, the bank has implemented an unusual system of "social collateral," which requires its borrowers to form groups of five people from similar circumstances. Each group receives collective funds, and group members are given the task of supervising each other. Essentially, each member becomes morally bound to the bank's terms by peer pressure. "Group borrowing creates solidarity and offsets the unpredictable nature of individual borrowers. In addition, because our loans are approved not only by the bank but by individual borrowers, women in each center [borrower group] have a feeling of ownership and competition that drives them to excel," says Yunus.

Grameen's system of agreement requires that borrowers lead healthier, more productive lives. In accepting a loan, borrowers concede to live by a moral code that Grameen calls the Sixteen Decisions. These decisions — ranging from "we shall not live in dilapidated houses" to "we shall plan to keep our families small" and "we shall educate our children" — urge borrowers to change the long-held patterns of behavior that prolong national instability. "With enough women agreeing to live their lives by these decisions, we have raised a level of social and political consciousness that was not formerly there," explains Yunus.

THE SIXTEEN DECISIONS

1. We shall follow and advance the four principles of Grameen Bank: Discipline, Unity, Courage, and Hard Work.

2. We shall bring prosperity to our families.

3. We shall not live in dilapidated houses.

4. We shall grow vegetables all year round.

5. During the planting seasons, we shall plant as many seedlings as possible.

6. We shall plan to keep our families small. We shall minimize expenditures. We shall look after our health.

7. We shall educate our children and ensure that they can earn money to pay for their education.

8. We shall always keep our children and the environment clean.

9. We shall build pit latrines.

10. We shall drink clean water.

11. We shall keep our community free from the curse of dowry. We shall not practice child marriage.

12. We shall not inflict injustice on anyone, neither shall we allow anyone else to do so.

13. We shall collectively undertake bigger investments for higher incomes.

14. We shall always be ready to help each other.

15. If we know of any breach of discipline in any center, we shall help to restore discipline.

16. We shall introduce physical exercise in all our centers. We shall take part in social activities collectively.

Grameen has also developed a system of checks and balances that optimizes the company's financial and social performance over time. Bank branches are evaluated and rewarded based on a five-star system, with the best branches counting the highest loan repayment and profitability rates and enabling the most customers to become educated and poverty free. To monitor the social and economic progress of Grameen families, the bank uses its ten-point checklist, which evaluates the degree to which each Grameen borrower achieves sustainable financial independence.

"We are constantly monitoring improvements in borrowers' lives. We check to see whether their children are going to school, whether people are improving their housing or sanitation conditions, and whether they have warm clothes during the winter," says Yunus. "These are our objectives, and we don't let them get undermined by the mechanics of what we do."

THE GRAMEEN BANK'S METHOD OF ACTION

1. Start with the problem rather than the solution. A credit system must be based on a survey of the social background rather than on a preestablished banking technique.

2. Adopt a progressive attitude. Development is a long-term process that depends on the aspirations and commitment of the economic operators.

3. Make sure that the credit system serves the poor, not vice versa. Grameen credit officers visit the villages, enabling them to get to know the borrowers personally.

4. Establish priorities based on the needs of the target population. Serve the most poverty-stricken people

needing investment resources who have no access to credit.

5. At the beginning, restrict credit to income-generating production operations, freely selected by the borrower. Make it possible for the borrower to repay the loan.

6. Rely on solidarity. Devise small, informal groups consisting of co-opted members from a similar background who trust each other.

7. Associate savings with credit, but do not make it a prerequisite.

8. Combine close monitoring of borrowers with procedures that are simple and standardized.

9. Do everything possible to ensure that the system is financially balanced.

10. Invest in human resources. Train leaders with real development ethics based on rigor, creativity, understanding, and respect for the local culture and environment.

COUNTERING MYTHS

The Grameen Bank's accomplishments defy skeptical contentions that microfinance is nothing more than a pleasant reverie. Since the 1970s, the bank has produced quantifiable results proving that it *is* possible to build a prosperous institution by serving the world's most underserved and overlooked people. Since opening its doors, Grameen has consistently achieved solid financial performance. With annual revenues of $60.98 million, the bank is growing at a rate of roughly 10 percent per year. It has made a profit almost every year of its operations, and of the $4.18 billion that the company has disbursed to borrowers so far, $3.78 billion has been paid back in full. Though Grameen's philosophy is philanthropic, its business model is financially self-sustaining. "We finance 100 percent of our loans ourselves," says Yunus. "Our deposits are more than enough to run a profitable credit program. We have not received donor funds since 1995."

The impact of microcredit reaches far beyond lifting borrowers above the poverty line. Microcredit builds stronger communities, fosters gender equality, promotes peace among neighbors, and has helped give millions of children the opportunity to become educated.

— Muhammad Yunus

To date, the Grameen Bank has lifted 42 percent of its clients, or 730,541 borrowers and their families, above the poverty line.[8] A total of 578,532 homes have been built using Grameen housing loans. Almost 100 percent of Grameen borrowers' children have been kept in school and the organization has disbursed 1,858 scholarships and higher-education loans to people desirous of attaining special skills in areas like medicine, business, and agriculture. In addition, through business and microenterprise loans, the organization has supported more than 2.1 million entrepreneurs working in fields such as shopkeeping, processing, and manufacturing.

Since 1997 the Grameen Bank has also been creating a network of organizations that provide customers with direct opportunities for self-employment. Grameen Phone, a service that allows Grameen borrowers to purchase cellular handsets with loans and then rent the phones with airtime to friends and family, for example, has grown into a $200 million business, having supported more than forty-three thousand local villagers since 1997. Today Grameen Phone has more subscribers than any other phone company in Bangladesh.

Over the years, Grameen's ideals have become a part of Bangladeshi culture. "The power of this system can be found throughout village streets," Yunus contends. "Women have raised their status, lessened their dependency on their husbands, and improved family conditions by having fewer children." Today the average Grameen family has three children, down from six in the 1980s. "Children are better fed and educated, the village streets are cleaner, sanitary and water conditions are better, and entrepreneurs have far more dignity and self-respect than they did twenty years ago."

In 1995 a national research organization determined that Grameen contributed roughly 1.5 percent to Bangladesh's Gross Domestic Product (GDP).9 Although today a comparable figure is unavailable, Yunus is certain that the bank's clients supply more value every year: "Prior to working with us, these people were not productive at all," he says. "Now they are starting new businesses and supporting other entrepreneurs. They are contributing to the growth of the nation's economy."

While these results are impressive, Grameen's influence on the wider industry is even more remarkable. Thanks to Yunus and his original vision, microfinance is now a global movement. Today 2,572 different microfinance institutions are operating in one hundred and thirty countries throughout the world. Collectively, these organizations have reported reaching more than 67 million impoverished clients, 38 million of whom are women and 42 million of whom lived on less than $1 per day when they obtained their initial loan. In Bangladesh alone, microfinance programs — including Grameen's — enable 2.6 million Bangladeshi people to move out of poverty every year — or more than 219,000 people a month. Throughout the world, similar programs enable 10.4 million people to move out of poverty every year, or roughly 866,000 a month.[10]

According to Sam Daley-Harris, campaign director for the State of the Microcredit Summit Campaign, microfinance's positive influence on the world's poor is grievously down-played. "These statistics don't show up in national macroeconomic data because such surveys do not count the activities of the very poor. They are not on the radar screens of the macro-economists, but [through microfinance] their lives are chang-ing," he says. What's needed to move the relationship between poverty and microfinance into the spotlight, he says, is more truth and less political banter. "We often use code words when we want to avoid talking about poverty. We say 'pro-poor' but don't define it, or we define it but don't measure it."[11]

In 2003 less than 1 percent of the World Bank and the United Nations Development Program funds was dedicated to microfinance initiatives. "That percentage would be dramati-cally lower if you were to focus on microfinance spending that reached those living on less than $1 per day. Why is this so?" asks Daley-Harris.[12] Both Yunus and Daley-Harris believe that the answer to this question lies in the resistance of business and world leaders to addressing the flaws throughout our sys-tems. Yunus frames the issue: "People will continue to suffer as long as we refuse to address injustice. Through microcredit, we have presented a new model and a new mind-set, with results too potent to be ignored."

BRIDGING THE ECONOMIC DIVIDE

While the problem of global poverty offers a clear moral argu-ment for humanitarians and socially minded enterprises like

Grameen, it also heralds opportunities for traditional Western capitalists. Imagine if 4 billion impoverished people entered the world market as producers as well as consumers. The economic potential would be enormous. Certain multinationals, like the $74.7 billion technology solutions provider Hewlett-Packard Corporation (HP), do not need to be convinced of the benefits of serving less-empowered nations. They are already well on their way to cornering the market.

"About five years ago, we started to assess the impact that we were having in the world — particularly in the developing markets where we have major sites," explains Debra Dunn, HP's senior vice president for Corporate Affairs. HP has a history of providing financial and volunteer support to a variety of philanthropic organizations worldwide and is a widely recognized leader in the field of social responsibility. In 2002 it ranked second on *Business Ethics'* 100 Best Corporate Citizens list, while the *Chronicle of Philanthropy* ranked HP as the second-largest corporate giver among U.S. computing companies and third in percentage of giving outside the United States.

However, despite the company's long-standing commitment to serving poor communities through offering volunteer time, cash, and in-kind donations, the organization's former efforts fell short of having the socioeconomic effect the company ideally wished to create. "We concluded that in the past, our philanthropic initiatives hadn't gone far enough," says Dunn. "We needed to take a bold new approach and have a far more major impact, particularly on the issue of the digital divide."

The digital divide, as Dunn explains, is a rapidly expanding global problem. The world's population is growing by 83 million people each year, and the poorest levels of society account for 90 percent of this growth. New technologies can't possibly reach the poorest segments of society fast enough, and so the poor remain poor.[13] Less than 6 percent of the people on the planet have accessed the Internet, while only half of the people in developing nations have ever used a telephone. Meanwhile, the technological advances of wealthier nations boosts their productivity at an ever-quicker pace, making the rich even richer.[14]

In 2000 HP decided to actively seek business-building ways to solve these growing socioeconomic problems. "Because we are a technology company and provide access and infrastructure solutions that connect people, we saw an opportunity to develop new ways of providing those solutions to communities that today are not technology empowered," recalls Dunn. "We believed that in doing this, we could accelerate both economic development and poverty alleviation in those communities and at the same time grow our market."

HP serves 1 billion customers in 178 countries worldwide. Yet the company only reaches about 10 percent of the world's population — the top economic strata — with its products and services. "That leaves a very large percentage that is not reached and for whom our current solutions are not really delivering a good value proposition," says Dunn. Today, five years after its initial revelation, HP's senior leadership is convinced that the most prosperous information technology markets of the future will come from the world's most underserved, underaccessed, and underprivileged communities.[15]

The company's leaders are also certain that they have developed a sustainable

> Writing checks is helpful but arguably a lot less valuable in terms of solving real problems or bringing the broader assets of a company to bear.
>
> — Debra Dunn

business methodology, called "e-inclusion," which simultaneously improves the welfare of humanity and the company's long-term performance at the same time. "We no longer view our corporate citizenship strategy as separate from our business strategy," says Dunn. "The two approaches are now tightly aligned." HP's e-inclusion approach is a model for the corporate world because it works to close the gap between technology-empowered communities and technology-excluded communities by making it profitable to do so.[16]

Since 2000 HP has sent some of its brightest employees to impoverished villages in countries like India and South Africa, where literacy rates are low, AIDS rates are high, and many people earn less than $1 per day. In these remote villages, HP employees have invented technical, educational, and support solutions — such as computer services, Web-based community portals, and training programs — that are specifically designed to help villagers overcome economic barriers such as illiteracy, insufficient access to new jobs, and limited ability to partake in global trade. So far, HP has invested more than $16.5 million on e-inclusion projects, creating a sustainable economic livelihood for poor villagers and gaining new market segments, product lines, business models, innovation processes, and valuable market intelligence for itself.

> We need a broader view of the role of for-profit institutions. Corporations must recognize that their primary role is to make a positive contribution to society and that profits serve as a means to this end.
>
> — Debra Dunn

HP's e-inclusion efforts have taught the organization some valuable lessons. The company has discovered how to optimize social change and economic growth and to compete more efficiently in emerging markets around the world. But even more significant, HP's experience with e-inclusion demonstrates why the assets of the business world are key to solving many of the social, economic, and environmental problems that our planet faces — and what the business world stands to gain by serving the interests of global communities that have been historically overlooked.

BUILDING A SUSTAINABLE MODEL

In search of the ideal foreign market in which to implement its e-inclusion strategy, HP recently set its sights on Kuppam, a remote village in Andhra Pradesh, India. This largely impoverished and mostly illiterate village at the center of a farming community of three hundred thousand farmers and migrant laborers seemed to present just the right set of conditions for realizing HP's vision. Many citizens lacked basic amenities like household electricity or running water, none had access to reliable technology-based efficiencies, and almost all desired a better quality of life. "Kuppam had all the right elements," recalls Dunn. "The community's development challenges were clear, its local leadership was strong, there was a great deal of untapped potential, and because we have a large presence there, the region presented a very significant opportunity for our products and services."

In 2002 HP's initial goal for its Kuppam-based initiative was to collaborate with local government, community, and business partners to decipher how technology could best be applied to boost economic growth in ways that were sustainable both for the community and for HP. Today that aspiration has matured into a highly advanced testing ground for socioeconomic and technological development. Through a rigorous methodology consisting of four steps — "quick start," "ramp up," "consolidation," and "transition" — HP has created a technological infrastructure that has influenced the region's ability to connect to the economic opportunities of the outside world so much that Kuppam is now described as the "Silicon Valley of the East."[17]

One would expect a tightly run organization like HP to enter a developing region like Kuppam with an incontrovertible plan for implementation. But as Dunn explains, this is not what occurred. HP's efforts in Kuppam evolved cooperatively, gradually, and in step with the local people's needs. "We had a vague outline at the front end, but the strategy and vision really had to come from the community and from the various partners participating in the project," recalls Dunn.

The first step, "quick start," Dunn explains, was designed to help HP identify and evaluate unmet needs. After sending a handful of HP employees to Kuppam, the company assembled a team of diverse experts, including local government, business, and community leaders, relevant NGOs, school representatives, citizens, as well as HP staff with technical, philanthropic, and government expertise. "Building the right ecosystem of partners is critical to succeeding in an emerging market like Kuppam," says Dunn. "Identifying the necessary core capabilities upfront, having the right fundamental skills present on the team, and making sure that we'd covered all talent and knowledge bases became critical to our ability to adapt to local conditions and execute effectively."

> We don't enter emerging markets with a predefined road map that we're trying to roll out. These projects are about empowering and collaborating with the community to leverage technology in a way that makes the most sense.
>
> — Debra Dunn

Knowing that the challenges, needs, and desires of Kuppam's citizens were drastically different from those of Western consumers — and that HP's existing services and technical solutions would not seamlessly translate in the region — the company invested a great deal of energy on an iterative research process. "We conducted visioning exercises with the core team to assess the community's needs and the cultural implications of those needs," recalls Dunn. "We also relied on third-party research, participated in immersion exercises, and maintained constant local engagement between community stakeholders."

This research process, although time-consuming, did in fact lead to the breakthroughs that the company and the community were hoping for. "Every time we unearthed a need, we rapidly prototyped a solution to it. We deployed that solution on a limited basis and closely observed Kuppam residents' experience with it. Based on what we learned, we would make modifications, allowing the solution to evolve — then we would begin the cycle anew."[18] Developing and then beta testing solutions to unearthed problems comprised HP's "ramp-up" phase and resulted in an array of people-centric technology products that are in sync with local citizens' desires.

INSIDE HP'S "QUICK START" RESEARCH PROCESS

"Our research approach consisted of several methods designed to provide us with a baseline of community metrics, so that we could capture business and community impact over time.

The visioning session was the first step in understanding the critical issues being faced by the community and taking the vision to action through identifying relevant solutions. During these sessions, the Kuppam project team was able to synthesize what HP knew about technology along with community challenges such as economic development, education, access to government or health care information, and capacity building.

Next, we advanced our knowledge of a rural community through the immersion of five project team members with local families for three days. During this time, team members interacted with the families, villages, and surrounding areas to document community challenges.

Our key findings included a lack of or severely limited access to basic technical services, a government hierarchy that had created intermediaries introducing costs and delays to service delivery, and the desire of constituencies to work and to support their families without dependencies outside their control. Problems like these all signified the community's vital need for technology."

One of HP's immediate observations about the economic circumstances in Kuppam was the limited availability of new jobs. Without the education and training required to initiate new streams of business, few citizens could find work in areas outside agriculture. HP's idea was to develop a portable, solar-powered digital camera to determine what kind of income Kuppam citizens could generate with such a technical device and whether or not there was a sustainable business model worth replicating.

The company "seeded" these cameras with ten local villagers, each of whom was given an array of equipment, trained to use it, and then sent to find work. Several of these villagers gravitated to local events and earned significant income by selling inexpensive photographs of event participants. Today they operate a thriving photography business that creates photo IDs and documents local events. "The additional source of income means a better education for their children and access to basic amenities," says Dunn. "But even more important, this experience has instilled a profound sense of self-confidence. Today these villagers are achieving things they had previously considered impossible. They are producing new streams of income for themselves, they are applying for loans to expand their businesses, and they are making a more significant contribution to their communities. They seem to feel as if they can tackle the world."

A similar story unfolded when a local entrepreneur running an information center began to use a projector and HP computer together to create a cinema. He now charges admission and offers local people the opportunity to view programs and films that were previously inaccessible. "We're helping members of the community unleash their own creativity around what technology can do," says Dunn. "They get to play with things we take for granted and figure out ways to use them that are relevant to them, while tapping into the technical expertise from HP."[19]

Innovations designed to serve the local farming community evolved as well. Because Kuppam is a spread-out area, farmers traditionally had difficulty finding resources that supported productivity. To obtain something as simple as a grant application, for instance, it was fairly typical for farmers to have to travel for hours to the local government office, deal with bureaucratic runaround, and then pay a stiff application fee. In response to these challenges, HP developed a Web-based program enabling farmers to access required government forms online and to tap into an email-based agricultural advisory board. The solution helps farmers to save time, to solve problems quickly, and to operate more efficiently.

These experiences have greatly enhanced the community's taste for business, not to mention the company's affinity for innovation. "We are constantly learning how to service new segments of the market that we haven't worked with in the past. And as a result, we've uncovered new prototypes, new multiuser solutions, and new business models that are not typical in the developed world," says Dunn. "These are great accomplishments for our business organization because they enable us to find new ways of delivering value in areas where we historically haven't had this kind of deep access."

After two years of developing and testing technical prototypes and services, HP was ready to begin working with local partners in determining which solutions were effective enough to execute more broadly across Kuppam and other markets, and which were worth phasing out. This "consolidation" phase has resulted in the deployment of a "total solutions" technical platform that includes a two-megabit-per-second network, multiple community informa-

> There are many assets, approaches, tools, and processes embedded in a company like HP. The trick was to leverage these while adapting our framework to a totally different set of conditions.
>
> — Debra Dunn

tion centers, a host of online services, and a mobile wireless infrastructure. As a whole, this platform makes the region more competitive and attracts new technology and infrastructure companies to develop additional solutions for the area. "We expect that the benefits of HP's initial actions will be greatly multiplied by the organizations that leverage the platform," says Dunn.[20]

HP'S RESPONSIVE TECHNICAL PLATFORM	
UNCOVERED NEED	SOLUTION
LIMITED TELECOMMUNICATIONS INFRASTRUCTURE	Basic two-megabit-per-second network, plus a wireless (802.11b) infrastructure that adapts to local electricity and living conditions and enables community-wide Internet access and services
LIMITED OR NO ACCESS TO AFFORDABLE INTERNET SERVICES AND COMPUTING DEVICES	Multiuser computing device with low cost of ownership, plus affordable mobile computing units for personal and professional use. Multiple community information centers offering pay-per-use Internet and computer access
LIMITED ACCESS TO CRITICAL INFORMATION AND RESOURCES	Web-based community portal that contains pertinent information on topics like employment, health care, and agriculture and provides educational and government assistance
FEW NEW JOB OR ENTREPRENEURIAL OPPORTUNITIES	Portable and energy-efficient technical devices that enable entrepreneurial opportunities, such as the solar-powered mobile photo studio
LOW EDUCATION LEVELS AND LITTLE AVAILABLE TRAINING	Literacy and skills development offered through touch screens and voice-recognition software
LANGUAGE BARRIERS OWING TO MULTIPLE LOCAL DIALECTS	Language-translation software, offered in three local languages, applied to Web-based community and government portals
LITTLE OR NO COMPUTER LITERACY IN SCHOOLS	Computers, Internet access, and educational tools offered to local schools

Another reason that HP's Kuppam project has worked so well is that the company intended eventually to relinquish ownership of the project. When HP entered Kuppam, it had a three-year time frame in mind. The idea was to lay the groundwork, obtain participation from local partners, and then transfer knowledge, skills, and ownership over to local leaders with a vested interest in the project. The company also envisioned a revenue-sharing model that would enable local partners and entrepreneurs to reap financial rewards for themselves and thus to move the project forward. These steps, part of HP's "transition" phase, are currently in the process of unfolding. Their successful implementation will be equally critical to the region's ability to transform itself and the company's ability to replicate the model across other developing regions.

DUNN'S TIPS FOR CREATING SUCCESS IN DEVELOPING NATIONS

1. Be thoroughly committed to making a positive contribution to the community. This commitment will build goodwill and enhance your ability to be effective.

2. Find the right partners. It is essential to assemble a well-rounded team and to attract partners who are willing to work together and unify around a common goal. This requires a level of team and trust building that takes some effort to achieve.

3. Identify the gap between what local people need and what you offer. There is a significant learning curve in developing nations, so investing in upfront research and directly engaging with local citizens and partners to evaluate gaps is critical.

4. Identify a sustainable economic model. The best solutions simultaneously deliver significant value to the community and build value for your organization.

5. Work with project stakeholders to define clear and measurable goals and mechanisms for reporting. Leverage your organization's project management skills, but be open to new ways of working.

6. Set up a governing system that allows stakeholders to collaborate and communicate successfully. The best approaches allow the right people to have input into the right decisions, without making it impossible to move forward at a reasonable speed.

7. Define a time line and specific targets with associated deadlines. Otherwise, it's easy to get bogged down in debating various alternatives without a lot of forward movement.

PROVIDING MEANS FOR ADVANCEMENT

Though HP's Kuppam project is still under way, the socioeconomic impact of the company's investment is plainly observable today. Scattered along its dusty streets are bustling government offices, community centers, schools, service organizations, and community Internet centers — all powered by HP technology. There are also new Web-based services that bring residents closer together and put them more in touch with the outside world.

Community groups such as farmers, working women, and entrepreneurs, for example, are now able to build an increasing knowledge base through email forums. Wage laborers can find work more quickly through an online employment exchange. Local schoolchildren have the ability to connect with other students from around the world and to access valuable educational information using the Internet. Parents can easily obtain health information through a Web-based community portal. Citizens can more easily obtain government services and forms through a new government website. Civic and business leaders can more efficiently manage their operations using basic office software. And the illiterate can learn to read through engaging touch screen programs.

"What's most striking is the level of ingenuity that has emerged as a result of the community's new experience with technology," says Dunn. "Local people have developed the self-confidence and skills that will keep Kuppam's economy progressing long after HP representatives have left." HP estimates that its training reaches more than two hundred individuals a week. That means a more sophisticated workforce and a more attractive market for Western companies interested in building on HP's infrastructure.

Recently companies including Analog Devices, World Links, and Digital Partners have entered Kuppam to deliver additional technology, information, and services to local residents. In addition, owing to an increased awareness of local conditions, nonprofit organizations such as World Corps have aligned with HP's initiative in an effort to address basic challenges like illiteracy, high AIDS rates, and poor water quality. "This project has managed to attract some high-profile partners who are poised to effectively address the unique challenges and opportunities in Kuppam," says Dunn. "In addition, it has resulted in a foundation that poises us to be *the* market leader in developing markets."

> The fundamental role of HP is to make a positive difference in the world. But to do that, we need to make a profit. In Kuppam, we discovered a better way to do both.
>
> — Debra Dunn

Today HP is far ahead of competing technology firms that are just assembling plans for expansion into developing markets. As Dunn professes, the Kuppam experience has proven invaluable for the company. "We've gained an in-depth consumer understanding and a far better handle on what it takes to effectively deal with the unique conditions of developing markets. We've also unleashed a solution innovation process that enables us to deliver more influential products and services across the globe." This new process has led to products like the solar-powered Mobile Photography Studio and various other multiuser computing devices, as well as fee-for-service business models that represent significant new avenues for profitability and business growth.

In the process of adapting to radically new environments, HP has strengthened its workforce. According to Dunn, leadership development and team building are happy side effects for the HP representatives engaged in the Kuppam project and in the company's e-inclusion projects overall. HP's commitment to bridging the technical divide instills a similar sense of commitment in employees who want to be a part of an organization engaged in bettering the world.

Today HP's e-inclusion programs are being executed in diverse regions of the world — from Mogalakwena, South Africa, to San Diego, California. In every case the company's collaborative, community-oriented approach has enabled participating regions to advance culturally and economically. And as Dunn attests, the company is not shy about disclosing the strategy and tactics that drive these results: "It's an approach that we hope to share with the larger global community for the greater benefit of everyone."

A NEW ROLE FOR MULTINATIONALS

When companies do business in developing nations, they have a chance to make a larger than usual contribution. Some are asking themselves, "What can we possibly do to improve circumstances in underprivileged communities? How can we best provide people with the resources they need to thrive?" Although questions like these burgeon, the strategic breakthroughs required to drive irreversible business and socioeconomic progress are hard to pin down.

The difference between companies that thrive by improving the world and those that don't is simply a matter of approach. More effective organizations create change by treating the world's problems less like a charity and more like a business. In serving the poor, neither Grameen nor HP launched a donation program. Instead, they transformed good intentions into enlightened business strategies. Both recognized that by creating a better livelihood for the poor, they too could prosper. And through using results-driven methodologies, both created a lasting cycle of prosperity.

Ultimately, the factor most responsible for the success of both programs was cooperation. Instead of imposing new economic models on indigenous communities, both Grameen and HP gave the local community — including the poor — a voice. They listened carefully to existing concerns and tailored every solution to these needs. Furthermore, both companies provided local people with a vested interest in the success of the project. Grameen's borrowers were literally given ownership of the bank. They were also trusted to repay their loans and to help ensure that their peers did the same. Similarly, HP's Kuppam project was built on a foundation of partnerships. The company conducted in-depth research as a way to build tools that people desired and then handed the program over to local leaders during the project's final phase.

Both Yunus and Dunn expect to see more organizations

implementing programs that combine the discipline and intellect of the business sector with a level of sensitivity and cooperation most often found in the social sector. "These two spheres have been excessively compartmentalized in the past, limiting potential on both sides," says Dunn. "I frankly don't subscribe to the view that companies are only about generating maximum profit, or that nonprofits are exclusively about the public good. Finding a clear social mission and a sustainable economic model is vital to both types of organizations." Yunus agrees: "Rather than be willed by greed, businesses must operate with a greater level of compassion, while social organizations must find ways to become more secure and financially attractive to investors. This is for their own good, as well as for the good of everyone."

HOW ARE SOCIAL ENTERPRISES CHANGING THE FACE OF BUSINESS, AND VICE VERSA?	
MUHAMMAD YUNUS	DEBRA DUNN
"A new trend is unfolding that merges the best of two worlds. Market-oriented social enterprises, a new type of organization, will balance out the current rifts between social and profit-driven enterprises. Profit-driven organizations will grow to understand the value of supporting a social cause, while social organizations will create financially sustainable models. We will eventually have an exciting new system that creates a healthier economy.

    We should be teaching this in our business schools so that young people can prepare themselves. Many business schools perpetuate an older mind-set that says that a company should take advantage of others for its own exclusive gain. I would like to put an end to that. This is the time for a new mentality and a new generation of business leaders." | "I believe that we are experiencing a broad evolution with regard to the historic difference between social and profit-driven organizations. In the future, there will be less of a gap between the two. There are so many business opportunities related to solving social problems, and I'm encouraged to see more social entrepreneurs with viable business models entering the marketplace.

    People in the business world have incredible skills and capabilities, and these assets will help define what social institutions of the future might look like. In the future more of the attributes that we tend to think of as particularly successful in the business environment will thrive within institutions that are primarily driven to improve the societies in which we live." |

EPILOGUE

Evolution transcends and includes.
It incorporates and goes beyond.

— **Ken Wilber**

Every system is destined to work against its givens. This is the point of evolution, which is essentially a constant struggle to establish new limits and then to transcend them, to move beyond them into more encompassing and integrative holistic modes. Wilbur's theory about the evolution of everything — from biology to physics, psychology, and religion — is equally applicable to business.

While the traditional role of the profit-driven enterprise was once perfectly appropriate, today it is becoming increasingly outmoded and narrow. Corporations are hard-pressed to find ways to exceed their old roles without simply erasing them. Though many of us possess an undeniable drive to redefine business principles, to seamlessly make a transition, we must work with what went before us. We must take creative leaps without abandoning the basis of the system. Evolution is a tricky balance. It "transcends and includes. It incorporates and goes beyond."[1]

About one hundred years ago, the structure, function, and purpose of the corporation underwent a similar transformation. Mass production was born. Product innovations led people to desire more and more things, and companies responded to the surge in demand. To make more goods on a larger scale at the lowest cost, they restructured existing operational models. They developed new manufacturing and distribution methods. They adapted new management practices and time frames.

The mass production movement gave rise to a new corporate mind-set in which productivity was the key to success. The environment was a lesser concern. In fact, it was thought of as a subset of the economy. The earth's resources appeared inexhaustible, as did its ability to absorb waste. The fate of future generations was of little relevance to daily business decisions. Thought processes were entirely left-brained: pragmatic, realistic, objective, numbers driven, and unemotional.[2]

Since the rise of mass consumption, the world has changed dramatically. Consumers desire more in the way of quality and in personalized service. Employees also have different expectations. They long for a workplace that offers more freedom, flexibility, and meaning. The planet has shown that its resources are finite, as is its ability to absorb waste. Technology, which enables greater efficiency, reliability, and productivity, has proven its value. Moreover, globalization has eliminated geographic borders, and global citizens have become more vigilant and better informed about the ever-increasing social and environmental problems we all face. The press, shareholders, and the public watch for errors of corporate judgment and progressively require more in the way of honesty, accountability, and responsibility.

Although the world has drastically transformed over the past one hundred years, the structure, function, and purpose of the modern corporation remain largely the same. The majority of the corporate world still relies on paradigms that were established shortly after World War I. Making profits is still a rule of the game, but what is the *point* of the game?[3] Most corporations have failed to address this question in light of the new demands of the twenty-first century, and therefore they fail to meet them.

All business faces a predicament. We know what we can no longer get away with. We have experienced the consequences of corporate crimes against humanity. Future generations will experience the consequences of *our* corporate crimes against humanity. We also know more about how environmentally and socially responsible behavior accelerates a cycle of positive benefits.

Ultimately, everyone working in the corporate world, regardless of vocation, has two choices. We can ignore twenty-first-century demands and continue with business as usual. Or we can evolve. We can operate in response to the knowledge that presents itself everywhere around us. We can embrace a new, more realistic mind-set and welcome its implications. Like any species or ecosystem, we must adapt to the new conditions, or ultimately we will fail.

Green Mountain Coffee Roasters and The Body Shop

reveal why this change is necessary, while Interface and BP demonstrate how the transformation can come to pass. Avon, Timberland, and Hewlett-Packard are taking some of the plentiful routes available, while the Grameen Bank, Eziba, and Stonyfield Farm characterize the pinnacle of twenty-first-century businesses' achievements. Beyond sharing a similar vision and mission, these high-purpose companies also share a great sense of urgency. They are desperate to encourage a widespread corporate awakening. They view the maturing of compassion as crucial to corporate survival, and they offer you their opinions, experiences, and tactics in hopes of inspiring you to follow their lead.

You can start by incorporating what you know and by identifying meaningful ways to take the next step. Address one thing at a time. Think about how philanthropy can become more of a strategic priority in your firm. Bring up a critical socioeconomic issue that's being ignored at a meeting. Assess the environmentally harmful aspects of your manufacturing practices, and devise a plan to eliminate them. Address company ethics *before* they become a problem. Tell consumers and shareholders the truth about how your products are made and about how you operate in foreign countries.

If these tasks seem unmanageable, then start with little things in your personal life. Begin to recycle. Research the social and environmental responsibility records of the companies you're invested in. Write a letter to the CEO of a misguided company. Write a letter to the CEO of a company that's mending its ways. Ask your grocer where he or she stocks the fair trade products. Ask your local clothing retailer how much the people who made their garments were paid. Buy an environmentally friendly product. Talk to your kids about the possibility that their soccer ball was made by someone their age. Talk to them about why it's important to respect all people and the planet.

The possibilities are endless.

If enough consumers demanded corporate compassion, no CEO would be able to resist. If enough employees within a company demanded responsive policies, management would have no choice but to abide. If enough companies successfully fulfilled a higher purpose, few competitors could help but follow suit. If enough competitors followed suit, perhaps the world's gravest problems could finally be eradicated.

Without abandoning our present system, we must all find ways to transcend it.

NOTES

INTRODUCTION. THE RISE OF THE HIGH-PURPOSE COMPANY

1. Though this point is clearly demonstrated in each of our case studies, the observation was first made by Harvard University's Lynn Sharp Paine in *Value Shift: Why Companies Must Merge Social and Financial Imperatives to Achieve Superior Performance* (New York: McGraw-Hill, 2003).
2. A similar view was put forth by Dr. Muhammad Yunus in his speech on Millennium Development Goals (Commonwealth Lecture, London, England, March 12, 2003). Trademarks and copyright reserved by Grameen Communications.

CHAPTER 1. CHANGING FACE

1. Ray Anderson, "A Call for Systemic Change" (speech, National Conference on Sciences, Policy and the Environment, Washington, D.C., January 31, 2003).
2. Ray Anderson, "The Journey from There to Here: The Eco-Odyssey of a CEO" (speech to his European contingent, originally delivered as a keynote address at the U.S. Green Building Conference, Big Sky, Montana, August 14, 1995).

3. Charles Fishman, "Sustainable Growth — Interface Inc.,"
   Fast Company 14 (April 1998): 136.

4. Warren Cohen, "Ray Anderson: Aspiring to Become the
   Greenest CEO in America," *U.S. News & World Report*,
   December 28, 1998 (accessed online at www.wjcohen.home.
   mindspring.com/usnclips/28anderson.htm, October 10, 2003).

5. Fishman, "Sustainable Growth," 136.

6. Ray Anderson, *Mid-Course Correction: Toward a Sustainable
   Enterprise, the Interface Model* (White River Junction, Vt.:
   Chelsea Green, 1999).

7. Ray Anderson, "Toward a Just, Sustainable Economy: Economics 101 Revisited," *International Journal of Corporate Sustainability* 10, no. 6 (June 2003): 8.

8. Interface, *A Better Way to Bigger Profit* (annual report, 2000)
   (accessed online at www.ifsia.com/results/investor).

9. Interface, *Business in Motion* (annual report, 2000) (accessed
   at www.ifsia.com/results/investor).

10. This number reflects the relative change through fiscal
    year 2002.

11. This number excludes energy used by Interface's Chatham
    facility, which it recently acquired. Since acquiring the
    Chatham facility in 2000, Interface has reduced that facili-
    ties energy consumption by 6 percent.

12. This figure takes into account the effects of Interface's use
    of renewable energy, rematerialization, and dematerializa-
    tion programs. The percentage reflects change since 1994.

13. Interface, *Business in Motion* (annual report, 2000) (accessed
    at www.ifsia.com/results/investor).

14. Ray Anderson, "Mind Set" (unpublished essay, Atlanta,
    Georgia, 2003).

15. John J. Fialka, "Global Warming Treaty Faces Host of
    Political Clouds," *Wall Street Journal*, May 27, 1997, sec. A.

16. James Gerstenzang, "Oil Executive Breaks with Industry Environment," *Los Angeles Times*, May 21, 1997, sec. A.

17. Leyla Boulton, "Oil Chief Presses Case for Solar Power," *Financial Times*, May 20, 1997.

18. Leyla Boulton quoting Greenpeace's Chris Rose, "BP at the Crossroads on Climate Change Issue: But Yet to Move," *Financial Times*, May 20, 1999,(accessed at www.greenpeace.org, March 1, 2004).

19. Glenda Chui quoting Chevron Corporation's Norm Szydlowski, "BP Official Takes Global Warming Seriously," *San Jose Mercury News*, May 20, 1997, sec. A.

20. According to a Reuters report issued after the Independent Petroleum Association of America gathering on May 16, 1997.

21. The $650 million in value was created between 1999 and 2002, primarily through additional sales of natural gas.

22. John Browne, "Climate Change" (presentation, Institutional Investors Group, Bishopsgate, London, November 26, 2003).

23. Numerical data drawn from BP's 1998 annual report indicating revenues of $84 billion and from BP's 2002 annual report, indicating revenues of $179 billion. (BP's 1998 annual report can be accessed at www.bp.com/investorhome.)

CHAPTER 2. ROOTING VALUES

1. Eziba, mission statement, www.eziba.com (accessed October 30, 2003).

2. "Investing in Tomorrow: Dot-com Multimillionaires Are Changing the Nature of Giving," *Success* (July/August 2001) (accessed at www.aglimmerofhope.org, December 12, 2003).

3. Since October 2000, *Forbes* magazine has consistently included Eziba in its "Best of the Web" picks (see

www.forbes.com). Eziba was also featured in *Time* magazine's 1999 Online Shopping Guide as "one of the best sites on the Web."

4. Although Eziba's primary retail outlet is the Internet (www.eziba.com), it also sells its goods through a direct-mail catalog.

5. Joseph Badaracco Jr., "We Don't Need Another Hero," *Harvard Business Review* 79, no. 8 (September 2001).

6. Joe Dolce, "Power Yogurt," *Organic Style* (May/June 2002) (accessed online at www.stonyfield.com/AboutUs/InThe Moos.cfm, November 11, 2003).

7. Dolce, "Power Yogurt."

8. Paraphrased from Martha Shaw, president and executive creative director of eFlicks, "Stonyfield Farm Launches Beverage Campaign with Soul" (press release, October 10, 2002).

9. According to the Vermont Economic Development Authority (VEDA). Actual net results for bankrupt or closed dairy farms in 2003 were not available as of December 2003, the month this case was written.

10. Governor Douglas's commentary derived from "Gov. Douglas Strengthens Commitment to VT Farms: Reveals Dairy Relief Program for Neediest Farmers" (press release, Vermont State website, www.vermont.gov, April 10, 2003).

CHAPTER 3. CO-OPERATING

1. Avon, *Relationships, Responsibility, Reputation* (corporate brochure, 2003).

2. These statistics reflect conditions among poor women with breast cancer. *Journal of the National Cancer Institute* 94, no. 7 (April 2002): 490–96.

3. Quoted in Sarah Brown, "Andrea Jung: Chairman and CEO, Avon," *Vogue* (December 2003): 176.

4. Timberland, community service website, www.timberland serve.com (accessed April 4, 2004).

5. From City Year website: www.cityyear.org (accessed April 8, 2004).

6. Harvard Business School Case 796-156. This case was prepared by research associate Jaan Elias under the supervision of Professor James Austin as the basis for class discussion rather than to illustrate either effective or ineffective handling of an administrative situation.

7. Harvard Business School Case 796-156.

8. City Year website, www.cityyear.org (accessed December 17, 2003).

CHAPTER 4. TRADING FAIRLY

1. Green Mountain, "Heart of the Cup," video (2Much Media, Burlington, VT, 2003).

2. TransFair USA website, www.transfairusa.org (accessed January 3, 2004).

3. A more exact figure is undetermined by the industry because most coffee companies do not publish the price they pay for coffee beans.

4. Green Mountain Coffee's Holiday 2003 product catalog.

5. TransFair USA website, www.transfairusa.org (accessed January 3, 2004).

6. In 2002 Green Mountain sold 15,569,000 roasted pounds of coffee. Of that, 42.6 percent included farm-direct coffee — that is, coffee purchased directly from small farms using

terms similar to fair trade — while another 11.7 percent was purchased under fair trade terms, in accordance with Fairtrade Labelling Organizations International standards.

7. Green Mountain Coffee Roasters, "Green Mountain Coffee Roasters Reports Fiscal 2003 Fourth Quarter and Full-Year Results" (press release, November 20, 2003).

8. Green Mountain Coffee Roasters, President's Letter to Shareholders, annual report, January 9, 2002.

9. Green Mountain Coffee, "Green Mountain Coffee Roasters Reports Fiscal 2003 Fourth Quarter and Full-Year Results" (press release, November 20, 2003).

10. Dale T. McKinley, "Shell: The 'Dragon' Must Be Slain," *Green Left Weekly* 522 (January 22, 2003) (accessed at www.greenleft.org.au, March 3, 2004). Similar opinions about and analysis of the relationship between Shell Oil and the murder of Saro-Wiwa can be found on the Sierra Club's website (www.sierraclub.org) and on Greenpeace's website (www.greenpeace.org).

11. Body Shop International website, www.thebodyshop.com (accessed March 4, 2004).

12. Body Shop International website, www.thebodyshop.com (accessed March 4, 2004).

13. Anita Roddick, "Who Cares about Social Responsibility?" (speech, Jacaranda Conference, London, England, June 24, 2003).

14. The Body Shop website, www.usa.thebodyshop.com. See the section entitled "Activate Self-Esteem" for more details about this campaign.

15. Jon Entine, "Body Flop," *Toronto Globe and Mail, Report on Business Magazine*, May 31, 2002.

16. CNN.com World Europe edition, Web article, September

18, 2000. (Article can be viewed at edition.cnn.com/
COMMUNITY/transcripts/2000/9/18/roddick.)

17. This figure includes cash awards granted in The Body Shop's
2000, 2002, and 2004 Human Rights Awards Ceremonies.

18. The Body Shop International, Letter to Shareholders,
Annual Report and Accounts, January 7, 2003.

CHAPTER 5. NEED CYCLING

1. According to the World Bank, 1.2 billion people from
around the world live on less than $1 per day, while another
2.8 billion people live on less than $2 per day. These are ref-
erence lines that the organization uses to define those living
below the "poverty line" and measure global poverty rates.

2. Dr. Muhammad Yunus in his speech on Millennium Development Goals (Commonwealth Lecture, London, England,
March 12, 2003).

3. "Twenty Great Asians, the Lender — Muhammad Yunus,"
Asiaweek (December 2002) (accessed March 15, 2004, at
www. asiaweek.com/asiaweek/95/20greats/yunus.html).

4. Daniel Pearl and Michael M. Phillips, "Grameen Bank,
Which Pioneered Loans for the Poor, Has Hit a Repayment
Snag," *Wall Street Journal*, November 27, 2001, sec. A.

5. Muhammad Yunus, Grameen Bank website,
www.grameen-info.org (accessed March 3, 2004).

6. Grameen Bank website, www.grameen-info.org (accessed
March 11, 2004).

7. Grameen's flexi-loan is an offering of the Grameen Bank
II, a new credit system designed to serve the needs of
those unable to meet the terms of the Grameen Bank's
basic loan.

8. This reflects 2002 figures, when the bank reached approximately 2.48 million borrowers with its services.

9. In 1994 the Grameen Bank contributed 1.5 percent to Bangladesh's GDP. In 1995, the organization's contribution was 1.3 percent and in 1996, it was 1.1 percent. According to the organization, more current figures on the Bank's GDP contribution are unavailable.

10. Daley-Harris, "State of the Microcredit Summit Campaign Report," published by The Microcredit Summit Campaign Organization, Washington, D.C., 2003, 3.

11. Daley-Harris, "State of the Report," 24.

12. Daley-Harris, "State of the Report," 10.

13. Derived from Population Connection website, www.populationconnection.org (accessed April 14, 2004).

14. Derived from Yasmin Ghahremani, "Heroes of the Digital Divide," www.asiaweek.com, June 29, 2001.

15. Carly Fiorina (presentation, Eighth Annual CORO Northern California Leadership Luncheon, San Francisco, California, March 9, 2003).

16. Hewlett-Packard website, www.hp.com (accessed April 5, 2004).

17. S. Srinivasan, "Box May Propel Communications in Developing Countries," Associated Press, October 29, 2001.

18. Debra Dunn and Keith Yamashita, "Microcapitalism and the Megacorporation," *Harvard Business Review* 81, no. 8 (August 2003): 50. Copyright © by the Harvard Business School Publishing Corporation. All rights reserved. Reprinted by permission of the *Harvard Business Review.*

19. Dunn and Yamashita, "Microcapitalism and the Megacorporation," 54.

20. Dunn and Yamashita, "Microcapitalism and the Megacorporation," 51–52.

EPILOGUE

1. Opening paragraphs contain paraphrased commentary from Ken Wilber's *A Brief History of Everything* (Boston: Shambhala, 2000): 5, 20–21.
2. Ray Anderson, "Mind Set" (unpublished essay, Atlanta, Georgia, 2003).
3. Donella Meadows, "Places to Intervene in a System," *Whole Earth* (Fall 1997): 8.

PERMISSIONS

Quotation on page 49 excerpted from "We Don't Need Another Hero" by Joseph Badaracco Jr., in *Harvard Business Review,* copyright © by the Harvard Business School Publishing Corporation. All rights reserved. Reprinted by permission of *Harvard Business Review.*

Quotation on page 85 from Harvard Business School Case 796-156, copyright © 1996 by the President and Fellows of Harvard College. Quote reprinted by permission of Harvard Business School.

Quotation on page 136 from a speech by Dr. Muhammad Yunus on Millennium Development Goals (Commonwealth Lecture, London, England, March 12, 2003), trademarks and copyright reserved by Grameen Communications.

INDEX

ABOUT THE AUTHOR

Theresa Vargo

Christine Arena is the former managing director of Polese Clancy, a former strategy director for Zentropy Partners, and the cofounder of several businesses. She currently heads an initiative that helps companies develop innovative and profitable corporate responsibility programs, and she lives in San Francisco.

FOR MORE INFORMATION

Many people have expressed interest in further exploring and debating the ideas proposed in this book. We strongly encourage reader response. If you would like to offer your opinions, view the opinions of others involved in this movement, or obtain more information about the presentations, seminars, and services presently available, please visit:

www.causeforsuccess.com